D0055290

# Escape from Nigeria

# Escape from Nigeria:

## A Memoir of Faith, Love and War

By Angelina Ihejirika
As told to Maudlyne Ihejirika

**AFRICA WORLD PRESS**
TRENTON | LONDON | CAPE TOWN | NAIROBI | ADDIS ABABA | ASMARA | IBADAN | NEW DELHI

**AFRICA WORLD PRESS**
541 West Ingham Avenue | Suite B
Trenton, New Jersey 08638

Copyright © 2016 Angelina Ihejirika

Book and cover design: Lemlem Taddese

Library of Congress Cataloging-in-Publication Data

Names: Ihejirika, Angelina, 1927- author. | Ihejirika, Maudlyne, author.
Title: Escape from Nigeria : a memoir of faith, love and war / by Angelina Ihejirika ; as told to Maudlyne Ihejirika.
Description: Trenton : Africa World Press, 2016. | Includes index.
Identifiers: LCCN 2016012032| ISBN 9781569024874 (hb : alk. paper) | ISBN 9781569024881 (pb : alk. paper)
Subjects: LCSH: Ihejirika, Angelina, 1927- | Nigeria--History--1960---Biography. | Nigeria--History--Civil War, 1967-1970--Biography. | Nigeria--History--1900-1960--Biography. | Women--Nigeria--Biography. | Igbo (African people)--Biography. | Nigerian Americans--Biography.
Classification: LCC DT515.83.I35 A3 2016 | DDC 966.9052092--dc23
LC record available at http://lccn.loc.gov/2016012032

# DEDICATION

To the memory of my parents, Raphael and Martha Nwa-chukwu Ishi, who brought me into the world, and set me on a path to get an education, thereby changing the trajectory of my life, at a time when the education of girls was unfavorably regarded and deemed a waste of precious resources;

To Mother Mary Getrude Nwaturuocha for opening the much coveted gate for further education for me and other girls of my generation at St. Theresa's Convent, Edem Akpat, Uyo;

To Mother Mary Lucy Enis, my very kind and compassionate Principal at Cornelia Connelly College, Calabar, whose humanitarian considerations made it possible for me to soar higher and higher in my pursuit of an excellent education;

To Sister Mary Thomas whose suggestion that I write a letter to my husband at a time of war and great uncertainty triggered a chain of happy events that altered the course of my family's destiny and opened the door to unimaginable possibilities;

To Professor, Dr. Christine Oti Ohale, I dedicate this book in deep appreciation of your painstaking efforts in editing this manuscript, and your firm correctives and suggestions that ensured clarity of expression and spiced up the story. Thank you, Christine, for your time, work, and the interest that you have kindly invested in this book;

And finally, to my beloved husband, Christopher, whose undying love, fidelity, and uncanny foresight have sustained me and my children through all these years; your death created a huge vacuum in our family but your memory lives on in our hearts.

# ACKNOWLEDGMENTS

This book was written in conjunction with and in tribute to the Ihejirika family matriarch—wife, mother, friend, sister, aunt, grandmother, village benefactor, and queen—Angelina. So many people have long wanted this story told. Thank you for your patience … and for your unconditional love for all of us. We are eternally grateful to the five American families, and the people they recruited for the sole purpose of rescuing us in our hour of greatest need:

Peter and Betty Dietz
Don and Janet Nevins
Jim and Helen Wolter
Jim and Pat Crisman
David and Margo Krupp
Senator Charles Percy
Judge Mikva
The congregations of Northbrook Presbyterian Church
The Catholic Church in Glenview
The Synagogue in Highland Park

# CONTENTS

# FOREWORD

*You have not heard it before, because it is an African
woman's story,
and our stories rarely are told.
I want you to hear mine.*

Nobel Laureate Leymah Gbowee

When food was scarce and the scent of death hovered all
around us during the three-and-a-half years that we were
separated from my father because of the civil war between
Nigeria and Biafra, my mother would hide her six children
each morning in a dugout covered by palm fronds, and go in
search of food. Though I was barely 4 years old, the memory
of peeking upward at a sliver of light through the fronds, as
sirens warned of early-morning air raids by the Nigerian air
force, stays with me. I still recall hiding in brush huddled next
to my siblings as the wide-eyed, barefoot soldiers in tattered
uniforms passed; I still remember fleeing with my mother to
her village across the countryside.

It is these memories, coupled with my mother's desire to
share her story, that have led us to write this book so that the
voices of the millions of African women and children whose
lives were lost during the Biafran War will finally be heard.

Maudlyne Ihejirika

# PART I

*When the British conquered the far North (of Nigeria) at the turn of the century, missionaries were barred from the area, and local rule left in the hands of the conservative Moslem Emirs (traditional kings). While the North was isolated from the winds of change, the mission-educated Southern tribes adopted Western techniques, accepted the possibility of change and soon demanded it politically.*

*Of all of Nigeria's tribes, the Igbos of the Eastern Region produced the most startling evolution... The last region to be penetrated by the missionaries, Igboland, took swiftly to education. Thousands banded together in self-help organizations and village cooperatives to help finance their children's schooling.*

*The Igbos were not content to stay put. They migrated to all corners of the federation seeking job opportunities in every tribal stronghold. Friction was bound to develop....*

New York Times
March 31, 1968

# Chapter 1 | MY HERITAGE

There was a time in my ancestral homeland when a man's wealth and fame depended on the number of children and farmlands he owned. Some men achieved this ambition for wealth and fame by marrying many wives. They also engaged in occasional inter-village squabbles during which some of their rivals were captured and retained by their captors as slaves. The captives added to the population in their masters' households, as well as working on their farms and increasing harvest which, of course, made their masters rich, respected, and famous.

One such rich and famous man at that time, about the turn of the 18th century, was my great grandfather called Ishi, from the village of Umuokoroukwu Ezeagu, Ezuhu Nguru, in Aboh Mbaise in the present day Imo State. Ishi married many wives, some of whom later became dissatisfied with their marriage and left after having a few children, while a couple other wives left as a result of co-wife rivalry that led to incessant fights among them. Generally, husbands did not interfere in women's issues, so feuding women were left at the mercy of the strongest rival.

Because polygamy was deeply rooted in Igbo culture, the first wife was mandatorily respected by all of the subsequent wives, but the last wife, usually the youngest, enjoyed the husband's favor, and was also expected to serve the head-wife or "Ishi Nwanyi." A man's eldest son usually enjoyed the privilege of having a head start in life by inheriting his father's youngest wife upon the older man's death.

Ishi's first wife had two sons, Nwachukwu and Uwadileke, and after his death, his son Nwachukwu inherited Nwangu, one of his father's wives, possibly the youngest one. Nwachukwu and Nwangu had five children, the oldest of whom was a daughter named Nwatuonu, and four sons, namely Ihuoma, Iwuagwu, Maduakolam, and Amamefule. The oldest of the four sons, Ihuoma, was my father who later converted to Christianity and took the name Raphael.

Ishi had a brother, Nwanyanwu, who also had several wives. One of his wives called Nwanyi had a son Peter, nicknamed Peter Brown, and a daughter Mary. Peter and Mary had also converted to Christianity, just like Raphael. Another wife of Nwanyanwu had a son named Ogbonna, so Ishi's family was quite large, mostly pagans, who worshipped the god known as "Ala Umuokoroukwu Ezeagu." This god, its worshippers believed, protected the entire village of Umuokoroukwu Ezeagu from poison of any kind, and the god's chief agents were the soldier ants. I recall an interesting anecdote about this god and its soldier agents: Soldier ants are black and big headed with protruding teeth and travel in battalions in straight or zigzag lines in search of prey. They would crush any prey on their path, and when they did, multitudes of them would form a mound over that prey, while the rest would continue moving until they got to their destination, which was the site of a poison. If any villager left any form of poison within the confines of the village, these soldier ants would instinctively know and would set out to find it. They would continue on their journey in a relentless search for the location of the poison.

Upon getting to the poison, they would surround the object, thereby alerting the villagers that something ominous was about to happen. Word would then be sent to the chief priest of the god to inform him of the sighting of legions of soldier ants. The chief priest would immediately send for a few of his right-hand men, and together they would follow the trail of the soldier ants to the site of the poison. When they get there they would disband the ants to see the object that was being surrounded. Since everybody knew everybody else in the village, that object would aid them in finding the perpetrator, who on being identified, would be subjected to severe sanctions, mockery, and shame. The fear of public disgrace and ridicule forewarned prospective offenders and helped to maintain equilibrium in the community.

My father, Ihuoma Raphael, was destined to be the 'savior' of the rest of his extended family. He was fortunate to have the privilege of a colonial education, and after his Standard Two, the equivalent of the American Fourth Grade, he was drafted into the army by the British to fight in World War 1. This took him to Europe and Burma where he served until his release at the end of the war in 1918.

My father's nephew Peter Brown and his sister Mary attended school in our village. Peter did well in school and duly completed Standard Six (U.S. 12th Grade), while his sister Mary had barely completed her first year in school when she got married. While my father was fighting in the war, his nephew Peter Brown became a teacher and taught at several elementary schools in our hometown of Mbaise. Although he was my father's nephew, he and my father

5

referred to each other as brothers because in our Igbo culture the terms half-brother, cousin, nephew, and niece did not exist; the natives called each other brother or sister, unless they were parents or elders.

Children and young adults did not call their elders by their names without using the prefix "Dee" for males and "Daa" for females; these are terms of endearment and a mark of respect, and are still used today in my own area of Igboland, and among other Igbo groups. That was why almost everyone in my village addressed my father Ihuoma as "Deemma," a shortened form of "Dee Ihuoma."

While my father was in the army overseas, his parents devised a plan to get him a wife. Being their eldest son, they figured that he would have to marry someone that they knew and whose family they endorsed. My father's elder sister, Nwatuonu, was already married with children to a family in Umuba Ibeku, a neighboring village about five miles from Umuokoroukwu Ezeagu in Ezuhu Nguru, Mbaise. As soon as she learned of their parents' plan, she told them about a young girl named Ebere, the daughter of one of her husband's relatives, whose good manners and enviable demeanor she had been admiring since her birth. That young girl would become my mother.

At that time, Ebere was only about eight years old and never attended school. Her father Onwunali was a hunter and her mother Nwanyi was a housewife who traded on snuff made from tobacco. She would buy the dried tobacco which she further dried on a very hot iron pot, and then pounded the tobacco leaves until the stuff was ready to be ground on a smooth, flat stone. She would grind it until it became fine like powder to which she would add a specific amount of potassium, and continue grinding until the mixture had blended, becoming powdery and ready to be scooped with the thumb in small amounts into the nostrils or ingested by mouth.

Ebere's mother was well known for this trade, and villagers trooped to her house throughout the day until quite late in the evening to buy their supply of good snuff. A small room adjacent to her kitchen known as "Usulo" was reserved for this business. Cowries and manilas were the currency of the day, and Nwanyi made a great deal of money from this trade, doing more business at home than in the markets. The big markets held every eight days while the smaller markets held every four days.

The floor of the "Usulo" was covered with a thatched mat on which the cowries and manilas were kept, and one would have to step on the currencies to get from one end of the room to the other. The cowries were like seashells, whereas the manilas were very heavy metals, and could not be easily destroyed. Ebere's mother was considered wealthy by the standards of her community, while her father was considered a successful hunter in his own right, as he rarely came home after each hunt without one or two animals to show for it. He would prepare these bush meat and dry them by placing them over an open fire for days until they were well cooked, much like today's grilled meat. Villagers would come to buy the dried bush meat from Onwunali, and this was how Ebere's parents, my grandparents, lived and survived.

They had other children besides my mother, a son named Onyekwere and another daughter named Maama. My mother, the oldest of her parents' three children, helped them out the most with chores. She observed her mother closely and learned her skill, and was able to sell snuff to customers both at home and in the market, whether her mother was around or not. It was this and her other good qualities that endeared her to many people, particularly Daa Nwatuonu, my father's only sister, whom my father fondly referred to as "Ada Nne m."

Shortly after Daa Nwatuonu's recommendation of my mother to their parents, the family went to seek her young hands in marriage for their son who was away at war but was expected to return soon after his discharge since the war had ended. When all the rites of native law and custom concerning marriage had been fulfilled by my paternal grandparents, my mother was released to my father's family by her parents, and she relocated from Umuba Ibeku to Umuokoroukwu Ezeagu to live with her future mother-in-law while waiting for the man who would be her husband for life.

In those days, girls could not pick and choose their spouses; marriages were arranged for them, and their parents' choices and decisions were final. Invariably, those arranged marriages worked out more successfully than marriages today. While living with her future mother-in-law, my mother learned much about what she needed to know as a housewife.

My father finally returned home following his discharge from the army, and was introduced to his young wife, then about twelve years old. His parents had warned him of her tender age which forbade him to go too close to her until she was of age, at least sixteen years old. So he left the village to seek employment and was hired as a Prison Warden at Afikpo in the present day Ebonyi State, visiting home periodically, particularly during his annual leave.

When the time was ripe, my father came home to get married. Because both of their parents were pagans, my father saw to it that my mother be baptized in the Catholic Church before their wedding, and she took the name Martha. My parents, Raphael and Martha, got married in the Catholic Church at Ezuhu Nguru, and thereafter, my father took my mother with him to his station at Afikpo. Their marriage was blessed with thirteen children, but only nine survived. Those were the times when infant mortality was at an all-time high, caused principally by either malaria, malnutrition, or both.

Of the nine of us that survived, five were boys and four were girls. My brothers were named James, Sylvester, Eugene, Lawrence, and Theodore, and my sisters were named Theresa, Bibiana, and Maria. Out of the nine of us, James, Lawrence, Theodore, Bibiana, and Maria are now deceased. Because my father was transferred often for his job, all of his children were born wherever he was based.

I was born in Afikpo on Thursday, August 4, 1927, specifically at 9:00 p.m. I feel privileged to have the details of my birth because my father had duly recorded them. Most people in my generation had illiterate parents and did not know their birth dates, but some had an idea only because their parents or a relative remembered an outstanding event that occurred around the time of their birth. People who were born around the close of World War 1, for example, could put their birth anywhere between 1918 and 1919, but could never be sure of specific dates. I feel blessed to be sure of mine.

Because my father was transferred often, my parents decided to send me to my maternal grandparents, the hunter Onwunali and the snuff trader Nne Nwanyi. So I lived a few years with my maternal grandparents until I was of school age. School age at that time was determined by a child's ability to cross her head with her right hand and touch her left ear. This was when my father, Raphael, sent me to live with his nephew Peter Brown, who had become the headmaster of a school.

# Chapter 2 | MY CHILDHOOD

The connection between education and social progress had been engraved upon my Igbo father Raphael Nwachukwu Ishi's heart as he fought on behalf of the British during World War 1. Drafted when he reached the tax-paying age of 18, my father underwent basic military training in the United Kingdom. For the first time he got to see how white people lived and interacted with one another in their own country. He noted that in the U.K. all children attended school, including little girls. So upon his return, he decided that all of his children would go to school, including all of his daughters, beginning with me, his eldest girl. My father began making careful plans for the first steps toward my education, as though he was preparing to send me off to a university.

Arriving home in Ezuhu Nguru, a village in Aboh Mbaise Local Government Area of the present day Imo State in the Eastern Region of Nigeria, he was hired by the British for a prestigious job as the warden at Aba Prison because he could spell, something he had learned in school before he was drafted into the army at the completion of Standard Two.

I will never forget the shocked expression on my mother Martha's face the day my father announced that I would begin my education by moving away to live with his nephew, Peter Brown Nwachukwu Ishi. Uncle Peter was the only one among my father's relatives who had also attended school. My mother, on the other hand, was a successful seamstress, tradeswoman and housewife.

I secretly hoped my father would hold true to his announced plans for me. But to placate my mother, I spent the next two months helping her around the house, instead of playing with my friends who also lived at the prison wardens' barracks, as it was called then.

* * * * *

Uncle Peter was a single man who lived in a bungalow-style house near the school premises where he taught in the village of Umuoti Inyishi. He was now headmaster of the primary school that I would be able to attend for free. Despite my mother's misgivings, my father helped me move in with Uncle Peter and his houseboy, Sylvanus.

Uncle Peter was as strict and stern at home as he was at school. I now know for sure that the discipline he inculcated in me contributed to who I am today, but back then I resented it. He had so many rules about going to school, coming home from school, and doing my homework. I also would not tell a lie. Uncle warned me he would immediately know if I was not telling the truth, keeping me on my toes at all times.

Whenever I spoke to him or responded to his queries, I called him "Sir" never "Uncle." We neither ate meals together nor did we ever spend any time talking. As a matter of fact, Uncle never spoke to me unless I was in trouble.

Looking back, I did get in quite a bit of trouble for not coming straight home after school, for losing my pencil, or for breaking an ink bottle. The punishment for all infractions was a severe flogging. Uncle Peter believed whippings were the best way to beat out bad behavior, and I got more than my fair share of that. He even made me select the small tree branch to be used in administering his tough brand of discipline. But I loved my new world of school and learning so much that not even Uncle's rigid rules or presumed unkindness could dampen my spirit.

Uncle Peter also gave me strict instructions to follow in the event we had visitors. Whenever there were guests, he told me, I must not show my face; I was to either remain in the kitchen or go somewhere else in the house. If he called me to bring something, such as a cup for tea or a glass for palm wine, as soon as I handed it to him I must disappear again. Uncle also warned me that if any of his guests spoke to me or ever offered me anything to eat, I must not take it.

One day my father made a surprise visit to Uncle Peter's house. It had been months since I had last seen him and I could not believe he had traveled three hours from Ezuhu Nguru to visit with us. I excitedly ran out of the kitchen as soon as I heard his voice.

"Nne!" he called, giving me a big hug. "Nne" means "mother." My father had given me the nickname in honor of his deceased mother, whom he said I resembled at birth and whom he believed had reincarnated through me.

I sat at my father's side as he ate dinner. He fed me food from the dish Sylvanus had prepared for him, and even let me have a sip of palm wine. I told him about school, my teachers and my friends, who lived in nearby villages. My father and I had an enjoyable time together, and I was sad to see him leave.

Although I knew Uncle Peter was in the house, I did not know he was watching us; it never crossed my mind to question why he did not join us at the dinner table. I learned later that out of respect for my father Uncle Peter did not join him at table. Shortly after my father left, however, Uncle called my name.

"Sir" I replied, walking into the bedroom to find Uncle Peter scowling at me. I had never before seen his eyes and face so full of rage.

"Did I not tell you never to take anything from a stranger visiting my house?"

"Yes, Sir."

"Then what just happened?"

For a moment, I was confused. Was he talking about my father? He was no stranger to me, but the look on Uncle's face was a warning not to argue.

"You embarrassed me in front of your father. You made him think I have not trained you to stay away from strangers. Go get my whip!"

I was too stunned to move.

"Go get my whip, now!" Uncle yelled.

I got the tree branch from the kitchen and handed it to him. Uncle whipped me so hard and so long that I urinated on myself, and then he made me clean the floor thoroughly. All during the whipping, I cried and sobbed, wanting to understand what I had done wrong.

When no more tears would come, I resolved to be more attentive to all the instructions I had to obey. Although it was painful for me to accept then, the lessons of following the rules, assuming personal responsibility, practicing self-discipline and paying close attention to detail had been engraved in my memory.

I did not realize at the time that, regardless of what I may have thought, Uncle Peter wanted the best for me, and I would later love him very much for that. There is no doubt in my mind that Uncle Peter's brand of tough love gave me a head start in life, and ultimately provided me with the wherewithal and resilience to save the lives of my family in a time of great distress. To this day, I refrain from drinking alcohol, even the mildest wines, and I still feel uncomfortable watching people consume excessive amounts of alcoholic beverages, as all that reminds me of that bitter flogging by my Uncle so long ago.

* * * * *

I never knew whether my father was aware that Uncle Peter whipped me, but he showed up unannounced again at Uncle's house a couple of months later. This time, I listened to their conversation from the kitchen: "I want you to resign your position and come back home," my father told Uncle Peter. "We have to make sure that our people no longer sell our father's land; otherwise we will have nothing to bequeath to our sons, and nowhere to go. Besides, I no longer want to spend any more money redeeming the pieces of land that our brothers have formed the habit of using as a pledge to borrow money."

"Give up my job?" Uncle asked. "What would I do?"

"There will be plenty for you to do," I overheard my father tell him. "You will set up a farm to breed and sell turkeys, pigeons, rabbits, goats and sheep. Until the business takes off, I will take care of both you and your mother."

I almost cried. If Uncle moved back to Ezuhu to start a farm, that meant I also would be moving back to live there. What would happen to my education?

"What about the girl?" Uncle Peter asked.

"Angelina will return home with you. She will live with your mother and attend school in our village."

My heart leapt with joy, excited that my father was going to keep his promise about my education. But as I was soon to find out, Uncle Peter had other plans for me. I never learned whether he discussed this other idea with my father, or made the decision on his own. Instead of living on the new farm with Uncle Peter's mother in Ezuhu, Uncle shipped me off to a village called Umunama, a distance of about fifteen miles from Ezuhu, but within our local government area of Aboh Mbaise, so that I could assist his sister Mary with childcare, as well as attend school.

Aunt Mary had a toddler and was pregnant with another child, and I was tasked with cooking, cleaning, doing laundry and taking care of her daughter, Priscilla. Both Uncle Peter and Aunt Mary promised I would still be able to go to school, and every time my father inquired, they assured him I was making progress. But my chores and responsibilities at Aunt Mary's house prevented me from sitting in the classroom for any appreciable length of time, and I never got promoted past Standard One.

It is now clear to me that God had other plans for me because Mary died in her second childbirth, and after her funeral, my father came and took me home.

"You are moving back to Aba with me, Nne," he said. "Go pack your things. We are going home now."

I was happy to be returning home to live with my family for the first time in five years. But more than being reunited with my family, I was looking forward to going back to school.

Uncle Peter's loyalty to my father was total, and both men shared a deep bond. When Uncle Peter found the girl he would marry, it was my father who bore the financial burden of his traditional marriage rites. After the ceremony, Uncle Peter brought his wife, Suzanna, to my mother at Aba to live with my parents. My mother, an accomplished trader and home maker, who also trained future brides for marriage, took in Suzanna, and trained her to cook, clean, and sew, until she and her husband were ready to wed. Uncle Peter's wedding took place at Christ the King Catholic Church at Aba, and once again, my father bore the cost of the wedding. Thereafter, Uncle took his wife back to Ezuhu Nguru, and they would be blessed with two children, Charles and Agnes. Unfortunately, Uncle Peter died shortly after the birth of his second child, but his family remained secure in the good hands of my parents and brothers.

# Chapter 3 | EARLY EDUCATION

Within a week of returning home, my father enrolled me and two of my male cousins, Dominic and Nwagbaraji, at Christ the King Catholic School in Aba. Nwagbaraji was the son of my father's sister Nwatuonu, and Dominic was the son of William, one of my great grandfather's former captives, who had become fully integrated into my family. William had two sons, Clement and Dominic, but Clement died quite early of epilepsy.

Since I had not advanced beyond Standard One so far in my education, the headmaster placed me in the Standard Two class. I may have been the oldest child in the class, but I did not care. I was in school!

The school's headmaster was Mr. Obinna from Emekuku, Owerri, whose son is the current Catholic Archbishop of Owerri in Imo State. He was a strict administrator, but also kind and encouraging when he thought a student was worthy. Mr. Obinna insisted that all the students be on time for morning assembly; those who were late received a flogging when the assembly was over. The mere thought of Mr. Obinna's floggings became my motivation to always get to school on time.

My desire to learn equally propelled me to become the best student in my class. Our classes were taught in English, but we had to learn to read and write in Igbo, using primary school textbooks produced by the few native teachers at Christ the King. Very early on, I was recognized as a good reader. That meant I was often called upon to lead the whole school in prayer during morning assembly and in the months of May and October when Catholic schools organized prayers in honor of Mary.

The priest in charge of the parish and the school was Father Groetz. He told us he was half French and half German, and grew up in the Lorraine region of France, in an area that bordered Germany. Father Groetz used French, German and English words whenever he spoke to us, joking that he was confused because he was from two different countries. It was under the watchful eye of Father Groetz and his assistant pastor, Father Stieggler, that I received my first Holy Communion and Confirmation.

My two best friends at school were Janet and Katherine, and although we were from different villages, we played together during recess. After school, we loved to play hopscotch, netball (basketball) and rounders, much like American baseball. Whenever only two of us were together, we talked about the one who was not around, and when the third girl heard what had been said about her, there would be a fight. This habit was common among girls in my school, but when my continued quest for education led us to take different paths, I never again had a relationship that involved three people because loyalty was sacred to me.

I loved school because it also afforded me a daily opportunity to escape from my mother's strictness and pressure to give up my quest for education. Like Uncle Peter, my mother Martha had many rules. At the end of the school day, my brother, Sylvester, and I had to meet her at the market across the street from Christ the King School, where she had a store. She did a lot of sewing, and traded as a retailer of rice, kerosene, eggs, tomatoes, and vegetables purchased at wholesale from farmers who lived in the agrarian Northern Region. Sylvester and I were responsible for carrying home the foodstuff our mother would cook for our evening meal.

I think the other reason my mother had us meet her at the market was to keep me and my brother from getting into trouble with our friends and the street children. When we were late, she would scold us in the marketplace and on getting home, she would give us a good flogging without caring who was watching, even in front of visitors in our home.

We always had guests. On a daily basis, our house served as a way-station for about eight or nine guests. Aba was the closest city to our native village, and our relatives often stopped at our house for a meal or to take a rest from riding their bicycles either on their way to the market or on their return home.

My mother was in charge of the Christian Mothers at Aba, having been elected to that position by the Christian Mothers' Association, and responsible for finding homes where soon-to-be-wed young women could receive training in the domestic arts of cooking, cleaning and sewing. Sometimes two or three future brides lived in our home for up to a year. While they lived with us my mother gave them the responsibility of cooking dinner for our family and taught them how to sew and trade.

I think being responsible for training future brides, some of whom were my age, was a constant reinforcement of my mother's gnawing concern that I should be focusing on marriage instead of school. Whenever I attempted to do my homework, or wanted to go out and play with my friends, my mother devised ways to get me involved with these young women.

"Go fetch firewood, Daughter" or "Bring some water," my mother would say.

She would then have me help in the kitchen as she supervised the future brides. While I still had my heart set on completing my education, I did pay attention to the lessons she taught them. I learned to cook and sew by observing the future brides and my mother. I particularly loved sewing, and I think I had a natural talent for it. Without any personal instruction from my mother, I soon was able to pick up scraps of fabric and create usable items, including dolls and dresses. This skill would serve me well later in life, creating for me the much needed opportunity to make extra money.

My mother, although a strict disciplinarian, was exceedingly kind and nurturing. She was very kind to members of my extended family, and continually catered to their needs, as well as those of their wives and children. She was the great rock on which my family anchored and a pillar of support for my philanthropic father. I remain in awe of my mother and her benevolent spirit which enabled her to perform a most noble deed for my family in a time of bereavement.

My father's uncle, Uwadileke, had married a wife who died in childbirth, but her baby boy survived. Not knowing what to do with this baby, my family decided to give him to my mother to nurture. Although my mother had come of age at this time, she and my father had not wedded yet, but she rose to the challenge and took this child and began to nurture him. So my mother actually became a mother even before she became pregnant with her very own first child, nourishing this little baby at her own breasts, as if he were her own. My parents readily adopted the baby and gave him the name Bernard at baptism.

Bernard was already my parents' 'son' before my own brother, James, and the rest of us came along. Bernard and James played together, went to school together, and practically did everything together. My siblings and I thought that Bernard was our eldest sibling because our parents never uttered a word about the circumstances of Bernard's birth. Many years later, after both of my parents had retired and returned to our village at Ezuhu Nguru, Bernard himself told my siblings and me the true story. His story is a testimony to the collective benevolence and humanity of my parents.

I still recall vividly one more extraordinary deed performed by my mother as it happened when I was in my early teens. This incident has stood out to me over the years, given that my mother had neither a formal education nor any kind of training in midwifery. One morning, a pregnant woman who was on her way to the market somehow entered the Aba prison barracks where my family lived. My mother was getting ready to go to the market when this woman sauntered into our house, having passed the rows of other houses before our own. Why she chose our house and not any other house on the block I may never know. Anyway, my mother, seeing her with her hands on her hip, immediately realized that the woman was experiencing labor pangs.

Without any ado, my mother suspended everything and focused her attention on this stranger, steering her to the bathroom. Within a short while, the woman had been delivered of a baby. My mother then called out to me to bring her a razor from her room with which to cut the baby's umbilical cord. This she did by measuring the cord to the baby's chin and then cutting it. Not long after the baby's umbilical cord was cut, it became apparent that the pregnant woman was carrying twins, and that another baby was coming. Once again, my mother guided the woman through the motions of birthing the second baby. The cord was again measured to the second baby's chin and cut.

Thereafter, my mother cleaned the woman and her twin babies and made them comfortable, offering the grateful mother a change of clothes, massaging her breasts to induce milk production for her babies. My mother went so far as to prepare for her the customary spicy soup for lactating mothers. All this was happening between my mother and a total stranger; my mother had not the slightest idea who she was. It wasn't until my father came home from work that day that he asked the woman about her relatives and where she had come from. This was, of course, before the days of cellular phones and the global explosion of modern communications technology, and so the woman's family could not be easily reached. My father later sent a houseboy on a bicycle to locate the woman's village and inform her people about her safe delivery of twin babies.

Three days later, the woman's grateful family came to our house bearing impressive gifts, all of which my parents declined to accept, suggesting instead that the gifts be resold and the proceeds used to care for both mother and her twin babies. Looking back now, I marvel at some of my mother's phenomenal undertakings and how her ingenuity had always saved the day from potentially disastrous situations.

My mother was the epitome of true Christian womanhood. She took on the stresses and challenges of family with exceptional grace, and her legacy, I am proud to say, has lived on in the children she raised. Whatever good deed I may have done in my life is a tribute to the mother that raised me. I salute you, Mother!

* * * * *

At age 15, I met the Rev. Mother Gertrude, a woman who was to have a profound influence on my young life. Rev. Mother Gertrude was the first Igbo nun from my area of Mbaise. She had been a princess, the daughter of the powerful Chief Nwaturuocha of Nguru, who was one of the few chiefs from the Eastern Region to be recognized by the British. She made the decision to jettison her life of privilege, preferring instead to serve God as a nun.

Rev. Mother Gertrude visited Aba in 1942 where I was living with all of my family and attending school. She was recruiting young girls for her convent, St. Theresa's, a newly formed boarding school for girls. After being told about me by my teachers at Christ the King, Rev. Mother Gertrude met with my parents to discuss the possibility of my finishing Standard Five and Standard Six at St. Theresa's. I learned later that she was thrilled to find that girls were already in school in her native Mbaise. At that time, all the schools were 'mixed schools' which meant that both boys and girls attended the same schools.

I will never forget that day as I watched my father instantly give his consent and, to my surprise, my mother readily yielded to the nun's proposal. In hindsight, my mother, a devout Catholic, was most likely impressed and honored by the famed Rev. Mother Gertrude's presence in our home. How could she possibly refuse the request of someone so pious and prestigious? Above all, my mother was happy that the convent would provide for me a safe haven which had been her greatest concern all along.

Whatever motivated my mother to cooperate with us became the catalyst for her change, and for a while she enthusiastically endorsed my education. For the first time, she was eager to help me arrange my supplies in the lone suitcase I had packed to take to school.

* * * * *

St. Theresa's was located in Edem Ekpat, Uyo, in the present-day Akwa Ibom state, some six hours north by truck from our home. The seven dormitory buildings on the campus of the girls' school were constructed of brick, zinc and wood. The mud walls were plastered with cement and coated with whitewash to prevent leakage during the rainy season.

Every student was assigned to one of three buildings, each named after a female saint. Each dorm had a large hall comprising 10 beds, instead of floor mats, lined up hospital-style against the wall. We stored our wooden boxes containing our belongings and treasured mementoes from home underneath the beds.

Our daily routine began with a wake-up bell around 5:00 a.m. As soon as we heard the bell, we rushed to the bathroom, which at that time was only a fenced out open space, using the water we had fetched the night before to bathe ourselves. All of the girls at our school had close-cropped, barbered hair, not braids, a strategy that was intended to help save precious time in the morning without having to worry about a bad hair day. After bathing, we dressed in brown, pleated skirts and light blue blouses, the handiwork of professional tailors, who had been hired by the Principal of our school and retained as staff.

We all had to be kneeling in prayer before the 6:30 a.m. morning mass, after which we would rush back to our dorms to perform morning chores. The next bell summoned us to the refectory for breakfast. If anyone was late, she would have to remain hungry until after classes.

Food from outside was forbidden in our rooms, but we still managed to occasionally smuggle food from home or purchase snacks during school outings. When we felt hungry during recess, or when meals were not enough to fill us, we relied on the fact that we could go back to our rooms and secretly feast on the *garri* we had smuggled in, mixing it with water, adding a rare cube of sugar, and Peak milk, when it was affordable, and with our fingers scooping the last bits of that grainy goodness into our mouths from the bowl.

The school assembly commenced with the bell after breakfast. The excited, squawking chatter of girls leaving the refectory marked the beginning of our classes, which we attended until 2:00 p.m. After dismissal from class, we returned to the refectory for our midday meal, followed by a well-earned afternoon siesta. The bell rang again at 5:00 p.m., requiring us to go back to the chapel to recite the Rosary. Following the evening recitation, we returned to the classroom to do assignments or homework until 6:30 p.m. Then it was back to the refectory for supper. Every student sat at her designated table, and each table had a head girl who supervised the sharing of the meals, manners at table, as well as the clean up after meals.

We participated in athletics after our evening meal and then began our next round of chores. Some girls would have to fetch water for the kitchen; others would be required to fill round earthenware pots with water to ensure that we had drinking water the next day. Every student was responsible for fetching water for her own morning bath.

I was extremely happy at school, although I missed my family and friends. Janet and Katherine did not attend St. Theresa's with me. Although the nuns had made every effort to make the school affordable, it was still difficult for families with lots of children to save the money for the fees, especially families that had sons to educate. I had to make new friends and eventually became close with an athletic girl named Dorothy Obiora. Like me, she loved netball, and we either played on the same or opposing teams. She was an excellent shooter and very rarely missed a shot.

I loved all of my classes at my new school. In addition to mathematics, reading and literature, we had religious studies. In one of my early classes, I was introduced to the life of St. Teresa, and I became her advocate:

*St. Teresa lived in the 16th century, which was a time of both turmoil and reform. She served God and left her mark on the Church and the world in three ways: she was a woman, she was a contemplative, and she was an active reformer.*

*St. Teresa was beautiful, talented, outgoing and courageous. She entered the order of the Carmelites, despite strong opposition from her father. Like Jesus, she was a mystery of paradoxes: wise, yet practical; intelligent, yet much in tune with her experience; a mystic, yet an energetic reformer. St. Teresa was a woman of prayer, discipline and compassion. Her heart belonged to God.*

I was very proud to be a student at this new school, named after a woman who was so close to God and believed in the power of prayer. One night following the recitation of the Rosary, I vowed to become strong like St. Teresa.

# Chapter 4 | POST PRIMARY EDUCATION

Whenever students were summoned to Rev. Mother Gertrude's office, they knew they were in trouble. I was quite mischievous when I was young, but because I was a good student, whenever I was summoned at Rev. Mother Gertrude's office, she did not whip me. She recognized that I was quite smart and felt I was acting out probably because I was not receiving enough academic challenge in the classroom.

Rev. Mother Gertrude would either ask me questions about my classes or create chores for me to do, making me feel that I was her best helper. The extra attention she gave me eventually led to my settling in at St. Theresa's and focusing on my studies, and helped prepare me for future opportunities.

When I finished Standard Six, there were few secondary schools in Nigeria for girls. There was a lot of social pressure for girls to marry and they were deemed lucky if they even made it to Standard Six. But the Irish nuns wanted to create opportunities for the girls to have both education and a family, and they decided to establish a secondary school for girls that they themselves would run.

In 1943, the nuns chose the brightest girls from each of their convent primary schools throughout the Eastern Region, virtually the cream of the crop from every school. I was very blessed to be called to Rev. Mother Gertrude's office where she announced to me that I was one of the 15 girls that had been selected from the Eastern Region for the inaugural class at the all-girls Cornelia Connelly College (CCC). Cornelia Connelly College, which was the equivalent of the American high school, was initially located in Calabar, nearly 100 miles east of my family home in Aba, and it would also be a boarding school. To reach the school, I had to travel in an open truck by land to Oron, and then traverse the Cross River in a pontoon boat. The trip would take at least one day, depending upon the weather. Although the school started in Calabar, it was later relocated to Afaha Oku, Uyo, in the present day Akwa Ibom state.

Even though my mother once again gave her consent that I could attend Cornelia Connelly, she still believed girls should be wives, not students. She quietly began laying the groundwork to end my formal education. Every time I was home from CCC for the Easter or Christmas holidays, my mother discretely put pressure on me about getting married. She shared positive stories about potential suitors, whom I would then decline to meet, or she would ask other relatives to "talk sense into me."

"What is this school about?" my mother would say, sometimes kindly, and at other times with indignation.

"I want to be a nurse, or maybe a pharmacist," I replied.

"Doctors use nurses as if they are their wives," my mother said. "Better to really be married than to be a 'pretend-wife.'"

My mother even asked my beloved godmother, Mrs. Mary Magdalene Odu, the wife of Boniface Odu of Amaohuru Nguru, to talk me into leaving school, but I would not back down.

After four years of pressure, my mother finally realized that she was not making any headway with me, and then turned her focus on my father.

"You have the boys," she told him. "Educate them and let the girls get married."

My father initially said no. He was the first 'educated' man in our village and he knew what education meant, especially for a girl. Even though his marriage to my mother had been arranged, he had grown to believe that girls were entitled to make choices. But my mother was a powerful influence. Proceeds from her trading contributed to the financial stability of our household, making it possible for my father to support his extended family.

> "Things would be so much easier for our entire family if Angelina stopped schooling and got married," my mother told him. "There would even be a dowry."

When it was time for me to return to CCC after the holiday, my father told me he did not have enough money to pay my school fees. He said he was already paying fees for several of my siblings, as well as for the children of his relatives. Besides my sister, Theresa, and me, the rest were all boys. In fact, we the girls were doing as well as the boys in school, if not better, much to my mother's amazement.

So my father's apparent inability to keep me in school was devastating news to me since I had only one more year to complete secondary school. But instead of giving up, as my mother had anticipated, I was determined to go back to CCC

33

even though I did not have the slightest idea of what would happen when I get there.

Upon returning to the school, I tearfully related my plight to my principal Rev. Mother Mary Lucy Enis, explaining that I would have to drop out of school. But after deliberating with the other nuns teaching at the school, the principal refused to accept that I would withdraw. She said they all believed I had tremendous potential and were all willing to create opportunities for me to continue with my studies. Because of my exceptional skills in Latin and Mathematics, in lieu of fees, I was assigned to teach first and second year students, even though I had no teaching experience and was still a student at the school.

Whenever my fellow fourth year students were studying Latin and Math, I would leave to go teach the first and second year students. I taught my students with my whole heart. Not being much older than they were, I was grateful that they were well behaved and very attentive to me.

"When one teaches a class, not every student will pass," Rev. Mother Mary Lucy said, attempting to reassure me. "What is important is that you do your best."

I have remained ever grateful to God, as well as to the nuns and missionaries from Ireland and America who worked at Cornelia Connelly College, for the gift of my education and the opportunity afforded me to become a teacher. Devoted to spreading the gospel of Jesus Christ and working for the betterment of our nation, these women also took it as their mission to raise us to become productive, responsible citizens of the world. I learned later that the nuns were overjoyed to have produced a teacher of native origin, who could be trusted with the same responsibilities they themselves held.

* * * * *

The new financial arrangement with the school shocked my mother, and pleasantly surprised my father, who later acknowledged he was very happy for me and very proud! I was simply overjoyed, having discovered that teaching was now both a career and my mission.

I spent a total of five years at Cornelia Connelly, graduating in December of 1948 with a Cambridge School Certificate, so called because the exams were set in Cambridge, England. I then spent two more years teaching at CCC, becoming the first full-time native teacher at that secondary school. Prior to my coming on board, it was only the missionary nuns. I think it was important to the nuns that the students had a teacher who could relate to them in a way the foreigners could not. I was put in charge of the extra curricula activities, such as sports and other social activities, which included interactions with the natives of Afaha-Oku, our new neighbors. Our student Girl Scouts interacted with the village Brownies and Boy Scouts.

In January of 1951, I enrolled at a Teacher Training College at Ifuho, Ikot-Ekpene, once again becoming the first Mbaise girl ever to attend a teachers' college. Nigeria is a vast country, and I am sure girls in other parts of our nation may have broken this barrier before me. Nevertheless, I was elated that I was the first girl from my autonomous community to go this far in education, finishing the training program in just one year instead of the usual two.

After overcoming so many obstacles to stay in school, and mustering the courage to pursue higher education, I adopted

St. Jude as my patron saint. I learned about him in one of my religious study classes. He was the disciple of Jesus who helped ordinary people understand that they could use the power of their faith and belief in God to triumph over seemingly impossible situations. St. Jude could easily have been forgotten since he was a backstage Apostle, unlike the Apostles Peter, James and John; but even as a close relative of Jesus, Mary and Joseph, St. Jude chose to serve his Master quietly until he gave up his life for his faith in Him.

With my new diploma in hand, St. Jude had just proven to me that he was truly the "Patron Saint of Desperate Causes!" I champion St. Jude and remain eternally devoted to him.

| Chapter 5 | MEETING CHRISTOPHER OBANI IHEJIRIKA |
|-----------|-------------------------------------|

My head was filled with dreams of moving overseas every time I heard my father recount some of his stories about life in the U.K., or met nuns and missionaries from foreign countries, or observed men who had left Nigeria for other far flung places and returned with a level of education and sophistication that I craved. I was not exactly sure, however, what "going overseas" meant or how to get there.

But the answer came after my third year of classroom teaching. Two other colleagues of mine had applied for and received scholarships to universities in the United Kingdom. Following in their footsteps, I decided to apply and, to my surprise and delight, I was accepted at the University of Glasgow, Scotland, in 1954.

While I searched for a sponsor for my studies in Scotland, my mother intensified her efforts to find a suitable husband for me. At 27, I was already 12 years over the traditional age at which girls from my village married. Every time I returned home for the holidays, there was an uninvited parade of men—from doctors to businessmen—seeking my hand in marriage. Some of them presented a comical sight—bad teeth, protruding stomachs, or they were too short! Others became intimidated after meeting with me, particularly when I told them I was not yet done with school. Those who thought I was an asset also felt challenged because my outstanding credentials threatened their African manhood. I was already the most educated woman in my village, which fact made these suitors think I was too smart and would be too difficult to control.

Out of respect for my mother, I met with all of the suitors, using the same criteria to screen them: "Do you plan to go overseas?" I would pointedly ask. When they said no, I dismissed them, but when one said yes, I tended not believe him. I was quite sure he told me what he thought I wanted to hear, but would conveniently forget he ever said such a thing once we were married. Then, of course, it would be too late at that point to assert my right.

Ultimately, it was the collaboration of my mother with Christopher's mother Janet that led me to change my mind about marriage. These two women, united in a quest to marry off their "older" children, invariably connived to introduce me to Christopher Obani Ihejirika, Janet's only son, who also was overdue for marriage by the standards of his community.

Christopher was from Okwu Nguru, a village less than two miles from my father's village in Ezuhu Nguru. My father and Christopher's mother, Janet, both grew up in the same village. When Janet married, she relocated with her husband to his home village of Okwu. Janet was her husband's second wife and had two children with him, Katherine and Christopher. But when Christopher's father died, Janet moved away in order to ensure that her seven year old son would have an opportunity to receive an education. Even though Janet never went to school, she very much desired for her son to receive an education by all means.

Coincidentally, Christopher eventually lived with and became a houseboy to my father's, nephew, Uncle Bernard, whom my parents had adopted and raised from birth, and who was then a school teacher in the Northern Region. By serving Uncle Bernard, Christopher had the opportunity to go to school without cost to his widowed mother, who depended solely on the meager wages that she earned by rendering domestic services to various tertiary institutions in the coal city of Enugu.

When Christopher finished Standard Six, his initial decision was to become a priest. I learned later that Janet begged, cried, and pleaded with her son night and day to change his mind. She could not bear the thought that her only son, whose family name meant "my wealth is my children," was going to become a priest. Over time, Janet managed to convince Christopher to change his mind. He then sat for and passed the entrance exam to attend the teachers' college in Ibusa in the then Mid-Western Region, now known as Delta State. It was a four year teachers' college run by male missionaries, most of whom were Irish priests. After successfully completing the course, Christopher moved to the Northern Region to seek employment.

He was soon hired to teach at the College of Immaculate Conception in Kafanchan in the Northern Region, a school run by Irish missionary priests. In addition to teaching, Christopher was the secretary of the Nguru Patriotic Alliance in the north. The patriotic alliance was a charitable association that provided financial resources and scholarships to indigenes of Nguru. Representatives of all the regional branches returned to the Eastern Region during the Christmas season for an annual meeting.

On Sunday, December 6, 1956, I was visiting Ezuhu Nguru when Uncle Bernard brought Christopher to my home. Christopher was in Ezuhu to attend the Alliance meeting, and I had traveled from Aba to see my mother and some other members of my family. Looking back now, I was somewhat arrogant in those days, because whenever my mother told me that someone had come to see me, I nonchalantly kept the visitor waiting. Not so with Christopher, for the moment I finally entered the room to greet him, my aloofness and cockiness vanished. I was utterly bewitched by his smile, his personality and his command of the English language. Prior to that moment, I never believed that a man of that caliber could be found in such a remote area of the globe.

I would learn later that Christopher was equally captivated by my presence as I represented everything he had been looking for in a wife. He, too, though long past the traditional age of marriage, was being selective and bent on getting it right once and for all. In no time, it became obvious to him that he had found his mate; in short, he had found what he was looking for.

Although I felt the same way, it was important to me to hold fast to my convictions and my plans to attend Glasgow University. I was disinclined to let this tempting suitor get in the way of my academic advancement.

"Do you plan to go overseas?" I asked him, just as I had asked all of my previous suitors.

Christopher replied with a question: "What if you find someone who also wants to go overseas, but wants you to wait until you can go together?"

"I know men can be very deceitful. They will agree to go overseas, but then they will not go or even let me go," I replied.

"I am talking about me, not anybody else," Christopher said very seriously. "Would you be willing to wait until we are able to go overseas together if you marry me?"

Christopher was educated, handsome and light-complexioned, with hairy arms. He was also a devout Catholic! Again, prior to meeting Christopher, I never dreamed I would ever meet a man from my native land that spoke English as well as I did. As I listened to him, I had to acknowledge to myself that Christopher represented everything I always wanted in a husband, and he seemed to be sincere when he said he wanted to go overseas. That was when I made up my mind about him, even though I did not immediately answer his question.

"It is getting late," I said instead. "I have to return to Aba before it is dark." Before we said goodbye to each other, he hesitated:

"How long will you be in Aba?" Christopher asked.

"I have only four days of my Christmas holidays remaining," I replied. "I have to return to the Western Region, at my post at St. Theresa's Secondary School, Oke Ado, in Ibadan."

"I am coming to Aba on Tuesday to meet with your elder brother, James," Christopher said. "I will see you again."

Two days later, on December 8, 1956, returning home from morning mass at about 7:30, I saw a taxi in front of my father's plot, Number 159 One Hundred Foot Road, Aba. I walked past the taxi without looking at the passengers, and went straight to my room. Moments later, there was a tap on my door, and when I opened it, Christopher was standing right before me. He must have left Nguru quite early so as to arrive at Aba that early in the morning.

41

"Come in," I said, welcoming him in to my room. "Please have a seat."

"Is your brother, James, here?" Christopher asked.

"James and his wife live next door," I said. "I believe my brother should have traveled, but his wife will soon come home from her nursing shift. You can wait next door."

Christopher did not turn around to leave. "Angelina, I have come to see you, not your brother," he suddenly confessed. "Please sit down so we can talk."

I sat down, caught off guard by Christopher's announcement of his true intentions.

"Tell me, do you have any plans for marriage?" he asked.

I did not have the opportunity to warn Christopher that my father was resting in the adjacent room and would likely hear our conversation. And just as Christopher began to tell more about his life, Dad opened the door and came in.

"Good morning, my brother," my father said. "Welcome. How is your mother, my sister?"

Christopher extended his hand and they both exchanged pleasantries before sitting down. I was not sure whether I should leave or stay, but I could not look at either of them. I felt stuck to my chair as I waited for Dad's reaction. Why had he called Christopher's mother his sister?

For a while, no one said a word. Then my father cleared his throat to break the silence.

"I overheard your conversation with my daughter," he said. "It is neither possible nor will it be allowed for the two of you to marry because we are related. Your marriage would be taboo. Your mother is my sister, and as an old man, I know our culture and will not be the first to go against it."

Christopher dropped his face in the palms of his hands as he listened to my father. When Dad finished speaking, Christopher spoke up immediately: "Papa, you and I are not blood relations. My mother is from your village; that I am aware of, but I know you are not related. So everything will be possible."

"I do not want you to raise your hopes," my father responded. "But you are welcome to go back to the village and probe further into the matter. Tell your mother to talk to her elder brother, Dee Moses, who also knows our culture, and will be able to explain the situation to you."

I could see the frustration on Christopher's face as he stood up to leave.

"Angelina, please postpone your trip to Ibadan," he said to me. "I will return soon with the answer, and we will continue with our plans."

Christopher knocked on our front door two days later.

"Our marriage is possible," he said to me as soon as I opened the door. "I have spoken with my mother and her elder brother, Dee Moses, as well as other people.

When my father entered my room this time, Christopher turned to address him: "The elders have confirmed that we are not related, and are willing to meet with you, Papa."

I watched my Dad as Christopher spoke. He seemed very calm, listening patiently.

"As long as I won't be the first to bless a union that is taboo, it is fine with me," my Dad said. He then stood up, and looking at both of us, he said, "You will have my blessing to wed if all is right. So you can both return to your schools until I meet with the home folk to work out the details of your marriage ceremony."

Having received my father's pending approval, Christopher and I became happy and relaxed, believing our future was almost secure. I walked with Christopher to the cab that would take him back to the village, and then returned to my teaching position at Ibadan two days later.

While waiting for the confirmation of my Dad's approval for our marriage, I went from not wanting to get married to not being able to wait to get married to Christopher Ihejirika. During this period of anxiety and anticipation, Christopher and I kept in touch by letter-writing. At that time, there were neither cellular phones nor the Internet, and the quickest means of communication was the 'Telegram,' which was expensive. Posted letters took a while to get from one person to the other, and this created long gaps in correspondence. Oftentimes, letters got lost in transit and never reached their destinations.

I once witnessed one such incident at the Marina Street in Lagos, Nigeria, as I passed by the Main Post Office. Near a dumpster, thousands of stamped letters were strewn all over the ground, practically left at the mercy of the passersby. These letters had been mailed from all over the world, but never found their way to their destinations. This was the fate of thousands of letters posted to and from Nigeria between the 1950s and 1980s, before the emergence of modern communications technologies.

# Chapter 6 | ENGAGEMENT TO CHRISTOPHER

While I was at my post at Ibadan, my father sent me a letter reporting that he too had returned to our village and had confirmed that Christopher's mother was not his blood relative. Eventually, after serious investigations by both families and village elders, Christopher's family met with my parents to choose a date for the traditional marriage rites.

After the two families had agreed on a convenient date, Christopher and I both arrived in Ezuhu Nguru in early March of 1956 for the traditional ceremony. But before the ceremony got underway, I went to my Dad and asked him not to accept any money as dowry on my behalf. My father agreed, but neither of us had any idea our decision had set a precedent. The payment of a dowry was an ancient tradition that is still being practiced to this day, particularly in the so-called Third World regions of the world. Bridal dowry includes the presentation of money, foodstuffs, fabrics, and wines for the sole purpose of marrying a woman. This whole ritual of marriage in Igbo culture involves an exchange of gifts on the part of the two families, symbolizing that marriage is a give-and-take alliance.

My father declined to accept the money when it came time for Christopher and his family to present the dowry.

"You would not be able to pay enough for my Nne. All I care about is that you two take care of each other and live in peace," he told Christopher.

Word that my father would not take the dowry spread through the two villages faster than a bush fire:

"Raphael Nwachukwu Ishi gave away his highly educated first daughter for free. Wonders shall never end!"

Some parents were so stunned they vowed they would never do such a thing. There were not many educated women in my home community then, and a high premium was placed on the few educated ones. A few parents, however, would go on to follow in my father's footsteps, having realized the deep implication of that gesture. Others would later devise a round-about way of maximizing their gain, by requiring the groom to agree that he would send one of the bride's siblings, usually a sister, to school, up to the college level. Waiving the dowry payment for Christopher to marry me conferred a legendary status on my father, and he was subsequently nicknamed "Nwachukwu Obioma," meaning "Nwachukwu, the kind-hearted."

Many people also wondered aloud why I had to marry a poor teacher, since some knew I had been sought after by doctors, lawyers and businessmen, before Christopher. All I could say in response was that Christopher was my choice, and I was not in an arranged marriage. I wanted a man of integrity, not just any man that had money to flaunt for all to see. After all, I had the means to support myself for life, thanks to God and my parents.

In a similar conversation earlier I had reached an agreement with my very best friend, Eunice Iyasele, with whom I taught at Ibadan, that we would not marry rich men. In hindsight, that may have sounded silly, since most girls in my generation were taught to dream of marrying someone rich. That easily ensured that they would be taken good care of, but that was not the case with women like me and Eunice who were independent-minded, as well as confident.

From our observations, rich men acted as if they owned their wives and hardly treated them with respect. They often left their wives in the house, while they sought the company of other women. We also observed that most women married to rich men never had their own money, and had to ask their husbands for every penny to buy whatever they needed, thereby sacrificing their autonomy.

We equally observed that men who worked hard for their money appreciated wives who would be equal participants in a marriage, in the hope that their combined efforts would enable them to soar higher and higher in their pursuit of marital bliss and economic security. With all of this at the back of our minds, Eunice and I both were resolved to seek a partner and a husband. I knew in my heart that Christopher would be that kind of man, and that made him the perfect choice for me.

* * * * *

The elders from both of our families assembled for our traditional marriage rites, many of whom had traveled to Ezuhu Nguru from far away locales. I would learn later that Christopher's family brought dowry gifts, such as lots of colorful wrappers for my mother, to honor her for carrying me during pregnancy and sacrificing her body to birth me. The prospective in-laws also brought yams, palm wine, many different kinds of drinks, kola nuts, a goat, and so on. They gave snuff to the men of my extended family, and a bag of salt, pepper and stock fish to the women. Throughout the negotiations, there was plenty of food, which was prepared and served by my mother and members of our extended family.

When all of the traditional marriage rites had been completed, the next phase of the ceremony then began, the part that thrilled me the most. My mother opened my door.

"Daughter, you are wanted by the assembly," she said. "Please follow me."

Once outside, I instinctively walked straight to my father, who handed me a wooden cup filled with palm wine.

"Take a sip, my daughter," my father instructed me.

I took a sip. Looking up, I noticed that everybody in our compound was smiling, but Christopher was nowhere in sight.

"Now, you must walk into this crowd and find the man you want to marry and give him this cup so that he can also take a sip," my father said. "Then bring that man back with you."

The laughter started as soon as I walked into the crowd, music blaring, to play the game of searching for my husband-to-be. Our family members shuffled around, quickly trading places and blocking my view. After moving in and out of the crowd for several minutes, I caught a glimpse of Christopher ducking behind one of his relatives. I walked over to his uncle, and looking around him, came face to face with Christopher and his bewitching smile. I extended the wooden cup to him, and he took a sip, never taking his eyes off mine.

Then we held hands as the crowd parted for us so that we

could walk together to my father, who was standing with my mother overlooking the gathering. After both of my parents had taken their seats, Christopher and I knelt in front of them.

"May God bless this union," my father said, placing his hands on our heads. "May He bless you with long life, happiness and prosperity, and bless you with many children. May they be the type of children who will love you like you have loved them; who will do for you what you have done for them. May God protect you and keep you safe. Always trust in Him." All the Christians responded, "Amen," while the elders stamped their right feet hard on the ground.

One by one, our family members each came up to bless us. The occasion was joyous, particularly for our mothers, whose prayers had finally been answered.

After the prayers, Christopher and I stood up and embraced each other in the full view of the gathering. There was so much food, and the people ate and drank, and danced heartily to the music for a few more hours. When the traditional ceremony was finally over, I headed back to my room in my parents' house since Christopher and I could not live together as husband and wife until after we were officially married in the Catholic Church.

"Angelina, where are you going?" my mother asked me.

"Back to my room," I replied.

"Your room is now with Christopher," she said. "You must follow his family to your new home in his village of Okwu Nguru, which is not far from us here."

"Follow them?" I was not prepared to leave my parents' home that night; I had not packed anything. "Did I really have to go now?" I asked my mother surprisingly.

My mother responded to the puzzlement spreading across my face: "It is the culture. You are going to Okwu now, along with all of the blessings that have been showered on you today. You will return home in a few days, just in time for you to return to Ibadan and Christopher to Kafanchan. You have just been married into your new home, so leave the packing until you return from Okwu. It is only a four day visit."

Without further ado, I followed the Ihejirikas to their home.

*  *  *  *  *

It rained very heavily the night I arrived at Okwu village, and Christopher's mother Janet readily agreed when I pleaded with her to let me sleep in her room with her. The rainstorm was so severe that it threatened to blow off the roof of Janet's small, mud house. The roof which was made of thatched raffia mats soon started leaking, filling the room in which Janet and I were sleeping with water. We had to get up several times during the night to move our beds. This so embarrassed my mother-in-law that she became absolutely convinced that Christopher had made the right choice in marrying a woman who not only loved him but also had the wherewithal to help support and care for her and her only son. That night, I made my future mother-in-law a promise:

"As soon as I move in here after our wedding, I am going to build you a zinc house so that rain will never fall on you in your house again."

Janet smiled bashfully, and I hoped I had brought some hope and peace to her poor widow's heart. I believed in my heart that Christopher's mother deserved better, and as her new daughter-in-law I wanted her to know that I intended to take care of her as if she were my own mother.

* * * * *

Christopher and I spent about three days in Okwu village before leaving to resume our lives. I returned to my parents' village home in Ezuhu, and traveled with both of them to our house in Aba. Christopher went back to Kafanchan in the Northern Region to his teaching job, and I left Aba and went back to St. Theresa's College, Ibadan, to share the news of our traditional marriage with my Principal and my fellow teachers.

The nuns and teachers were very happy for me, even though marrying Christopher meant that I would eventually leave St. Theresa's. Coming from an athletic background, I was in charge of athletics at the school; my brothers excelled in boxing, soccer, and tennis, while my sister Theresa and I were excellent sprinters. My sister Theresa was nicknamed "Train" because she was an exceptional sprinter, and I excelled in netball, rounders, and relay race. As a result, I was made a coach both at CCC and now at St. Theresa's.

By the time I returned to Ibadan, school had already begun in earnest, so I had to focus all attention on my students instead of dwelling on my future plans. Just as I was helping my students to settle into their daily routine, we received word in March of 1957 that Ghana had achieved political independence from the British. Kwame Nkrumah, who had once been a teacher, was now that country's first president. "Independence fever" swept across the entire continent of Africa and awakened much excitement in our hearts.

Despite not being politically involved, all of the teachers

51

and girls at St. Theresa's were enveloped in the pride, promise and possibility of Nigerians someday attaining political independence and governing themselves. It made each of us more conscious of the important role we could play in the development of our nation. As teachers, we focused more on making sure the girls got the best possible education.

My busy schedule at the convent notwithstanding, Christopher was never too far away in my thoughts. I pondered in my heart how we would ever get to know each other when we did not live under the same roof, but lived hundreds of miles apart. As if he could discern my thoughts, a letter arrived from Christopher announcing his plans to spend Easter vacation with me at Ibadan.

It was to be the first of scores of letters that we exchanged prior to our Catholic wedding. These letters did not comprise pages of romantic declarations, but were rather practical exchanges about our values and ideas, aspirations and dreams. Whenever I spoke my mind about my own expectations in our marriage, Christopher would show his displeasure by not replying at all. Still, no words or minor disagreements could alter our destiny as husband and wife. He reminded me a thousand times that he did not intend to cause me any anguish by his occasional silence or bluff words. I did not mind, I replied, because I knew, without equivocation, that I could always resume my quest to go overseas and make my way to Glasgow. Of course, I was bluffing, too. Christopher was too handsome to let my stupid pride get in the way, and the next letter from him was filled with joyful and loving words.

\* \* \* \* \*

During Easter vacation in April of 1957, Christopher stayed

at the home of Oliver and Anna Onyekwere of Nnarambia, Ahiara, family friends who were then living in Ibadan. He visited me daily at the convent, and to my surprise, Christopher arranged for us to have an official engagement party at the Onyekwere's home. I was able to invite my friends from the convent, and the host family invited their friends who lived in the area. We also invited people from our village resident in the Western Region.

There was plenty of food, good music and dancing, as well as lots of laughter, teasing, and jokes, all directed at us, the older love birds. Most of our friends in our age group had already been married for quite a few years, and had children of their own. Looking back now, I can honestly say I am glad I waited, and I am certain Christopher felt the same way. Because of our education and life experiences, we were mature and ready when it came time to forge a close relationship. Luckily, we both had strong faith in God, and this would ultimately help us to withstand unimaginable obstacles.

After most of the guests had left the engagement party, Christopher said that we needed to have a serious conversation. I was a bit taken aback by the seriousness of his tone, not having any idea what he wanted to discuss with me.

"Angelina, as I told you, I believe in marriage for life. No divorces," Christopher said.

I was not sure what "divorce" meant, but I nodded my head.

"I want us to have our church wedding ceremony this very year! We must set a date before I return to Kafanchan."

I almost asked why he was in such a hurry, since we were

already husband and wife as the result of the traditional ceremony in the village. I thought that waiting until the following year would allow us more time to plan our church wedding and save money for it, but I decided not to object. Instead, I smiled and nodded again.

"What is your favorite month?" Christopher asked.

"October," I replied. October was the month of the feast of my favorite saint, St. Jude. I wondered if Christopher knew that the name "Jude" meant "giver of joy," and that St. Jude never gave up hope in the face of untold hardships and persecutions. Not only was St. Jude a source of inspiration, he was also a source of courage. With St. Jude's blessing we were sure to have a long and happy marriage.

"That's fine," Christopher said. "We will get married in October. Do you have a favorite date, too?"

I consulted two of my friends who had stayed back with me after the party, Eunice and Miss Gilmartin, an Irish lay missionary, who taught at St. Theresa's with us. Miss Gilmartin was so excited about our wedding that she volunteered to order our wedding rings from Ireland.

"We have decided on Saturday, October 12th" I told Christopher.

"That's fine with me," he said, enfolding me in a warm embrace. "That will be the most special day of our lives. Now, I am happy and satisfied, and I think I can return to Kafanchan this weekend to get started on the wedding preparations before you come," Christopher continued.

He did leave over that weekend, and I saw him off at the Ibadan Railway station. The six months before I left Ibadan for Kafanchan seemed to be the longest months of that year because I was more than ready to be with Christopher as my husband, but had to wait a little while.

After my engagement to Christopher, my best friend Eunice got serious with her own suitor, Mr. Sergius Okeke, who was also a teacher in Zaria, another town in Northern Nigeria, not too far from Kafanchan. Eunice and Sergius soon had a date during the summer of 1957 for their own engagement. As soon as schools were closed for the summer, Eunice joined Sergius in Zaria where they celebrated their engagement, as well as set a date for their November 1957 wedding, one month after mine and Christopher's. Eunice married Sergius, a poor teacher, but a hairy, exceptionally handsome man, and six and a half feet tall! Ultimately, both Eunice and I got what we asked and waited for in life. Our two families had remained friends and kept in touch, even after my own family relocated to the United States, and Eunice's to Enugu. Eunice has six children – four boys and two girls, while I have seven children – three boys and four girls. The two families have had one thing in common: we cherish integrity.

# Chapter 7 | MARRIAGE AND EARLY CAREER

The wedding rings arrived from Ireland in June, just as classes were ending for the summer break. But instead of heading immediately to Kafanchan to focus on our wedding, I enrolled in classes at the Singer Sewing Institute at Ibadan to learn advanced sewing techniques and embroidery. I wanted to have another potential source of income to supplement my salary or in the event that something prevented me from teaching.

When the training program ended, I traveled to Kafanchan to prepare for our wedding. My very best friend Eunice and her handsome Sergius, now engaged, both attended the wedding. My mother soon joined us, but my Dad was sick and too frail to travel and so would not be there to give me away. My brother, James, who could have stood in for Dad could not attend either. In the end, Pa Edward Ufomadu, an elder from Christopher's village of Okwu, walked me down the aisle and gave me away.

It was a traditional Catholic wedding at Immaculate Conception Church in Kafanchan, officiated by the Rev. Father Hackett from Ireland. I wore a long white gown, made by my friend Nelly Okafor, as well as a beautiful veil, and Christopher looked resplendent in a dark tailored suit. The church was packed with people who had come to see for themselves that "Ever Young," Christopher's nickname, was finally tying the knot.

Some brides and grooms tend to be nervous before their wedding ceremony, but not so for Christopher and I; we were both calm and confident throughout the ceremony.

In addition to Eunice and her fiancé, my mother and other family friends attended the ceremony, along with Christopher's sister, Katherine. All of Christopher's previous intended were at the wedding, too, and many of them were quite pretty. I knew some people may have thought that I was not beautiful enough for my handsome husband, but our marriage had not been arranged; Christopher himself had chosen me and I had chosen him.

After the church ceremony, the real celebration began! We had traditional Nigerian dishes in abundance, and there was music and dancing of the Rhumba, Fox Trot, Quick-step, and Cha Cha Cha. Dancing was the one thing Christopher and I had in common, and we lit up the hall with our fancy dance steps. There were innumerable congratulatory messages and tributes, and finally, the village elder rose to speak.

"I know that most people judge beauty by appearance," he said, gazing at me. "But what I call beauty is the character of the person. That is truly what makes a person beautiful. Angelina, today I rename you *Agwawunma*, which means that true beauty is portrayed in a person's character. I know now that your character must have captivated 'Ever Young' when he first met you."

That elder lived to be 104 years old, and every time he saw me in Kafanchan, he treated me with the utmost respect.

＊ ＊ ＊ ＊ ＊

My mother stayed only one more day following the whirlwind of our wedding activities, and on Sunday evening she announced that she would be returning home to Aba.

"Mama, why not stay a little longer?" I asked.

"Am I going to marry your husband with you?" my mother replied.

I laughed, even though she seemed quite serious.

My mother saved her parting wisdom until we were alone at the train station. "Christopher is not a troublesome man," she said, looking me directly in the eye. "If there ever is any trouble it is you!"

"When the trouble comes we will see who started it," I replied. Obviously, my independent and strong willed personality did not disappear at the altar.

My mother hugged me and boarded the train, leaving me with that maternal advice to begin my new life with Christopher. Sadly, that was the last time I saw my mother as she died barely one month after my wedding. A doctor at the hospital where she had been rushed told my brother that she most probably fell into a diabetic coma. In those days, unfortunately, we were quite ignorant of the ravages of diabetes.

Sometime later, I shared with Christopher my mother's prediction that I would likely be the source of trouble in our marriage. It came up again during our discussion of his daily habit of playing the lottery, a habit he formed long before I met him. Sometimes Christopher won some money, but many more times he lost.

"I think you should stop playing the lottery because our salaries are not that much," I told him. "We need to save our money."

"You are right, Angelina," he told me. "I promise, I will stop."

But the truth is that Christopher secretly continued to play the lottery, and I discovered this one day while collecting our mail. I saw a letter addressed to the Lottery House in Christopher's handwriting that had been returned. I decided to open it and found a money order Christopher had purchased to play the lottery. Instead of making trouble, I took the money order to the post office and cashed it. Then I went on a shopping spree, purchasing quite a few things for myself and nothing for Christopher.

My husband was already home when I returned from my shopping, and showed him all of the things I had purchased, which he greatly admired. I could tell by his expression that he was also puzzled, but I waited for him to speak.

"Angelina, where did you get the money to buy all of these things?" he asked. "Your spending allowance is not..."

Before he could finish his sentence, I took out of a drawer the envelope Christopher had addressed to the Lottery House and a photocopy of the money order I had cashed to pay for my goodies. My husband was dumbfounded. I reminded him about what my mother said to me at the train station before she left after our wedding.

"Did I cause this trouble?" I asked him.

"What trouble?" Christopher replied.

That was the end of the lottery habit for the rest of our married life.

\* \* \* \* \*

About two weeks after our wedding, there was a big party at the Nigeria Railway station, which was located at the center of Kafanchan. Christopher and I attended this party, along with all the local celebrities and many of the young men and women from neighboring villages. Most of these young people were eligible bachelors and single ladies. Christopher knew many of the ladies, some of whom he had made their acquaintance before we met. The party was amazing, and I was thrilled to meet people from diverse cultures and backgrounds.

Just before the evening ended, the Master of Ceremony announced that there was going to be a beauty contest. Instead of having all of the contestants line up in the hall, the judges left us to continue dancing while they walked around tapping women on the shoulder to let them know they had been eliminated.

It was a tough competition, and some of the women in that room were real beauties who had sought to be Christopher's wife. Most of them were fabulously dressed and adorned in rich jewelry. On the other hand, I was dressed in simple, but befitting attire. Even my accessories were too simple to be noticed. After all, I had spent the majority of my life going to school and living in a convent, a place where conspicuous make up and jewelry were neither condoned nor allowed.

Eventually, there were only three ladies left on the dance floor and, to my surprise, I was one of them. Before the competition, I would never have presented myself as a candidate for the Beauty Queen of Kafanchan, and was surprised to find myself among the finalists. I waited patiently, expecting to hear my name as the next person to be eliminated. I studied the faces of the two beautiful women standing on either side of me. I was busy smiling at them, attempting to determine which one I would choose to be the beauty queen. Suddenly, the room was quiet in anticipation of the emcee's announcement of the winner. The result dropped like a bombshell: "Mrs. Angelina Ihejirika is the Beauty Queen of Kafanchan!"

Everyone seemed to gasp in surprise as the beaded crown was placed upon my head. Then like a wave, people rushed excitedly forward to congratulate me and Christopher, showering me with presents. The coronation was a reaffirmation to me that my husband really had won the heart of the most prized beauty, and the title followed me around for as long as we lived in Kafanchan.

\* \* \* \* \*

I was later offered a job at Immaculate Conception College, the same place where Christopher taught, because of my enviable credentials. It was a teacher training institute for male students. I was passionate about teaching, and loved being in the classroom again, and the boys I taught seemed to absorb wholeheartedly whatever I had to offer.

Nine months after our Catholic wedding, our first child was born – a beautiful baby girl that we named Winifred. My best friend Eunice, now married to Sergius, came to the hospital to assist me with the baby, and remained with us for about two weeks. Eunice was then about 6 months pregnant with her first child. I had a total of 12 weeks of maternity leave which enabled me time to finally get our new home organized and get the baby settled.

At the end of the leave, Christopher's sister, Pauline, moved closer to be with us. She was a teacher, too, but was able to arrange her schedule to enable her care for Winifred so I could go back to work. We also had a houseboy, Cyril, who had been with Christopher since his first teaching job. He was responsible for preparing our meals, keeping our home clean, and helping me with the laundry.

Realizing that it would be a challenge to support a family with a teacher's salary in a private school, Christopher began to explore other employment options. Within a year, he was offered a job at the government's education program. We had to pack up and relocate to Kaduna by train, a distance of nearly 130 miles south of Kafanchan, where Christopher had been offered a job at the Kaduna Government Training Center, a trade school. Not long after we arrived in Kaduna, I was equally offered a job at Holy Rosary Convent School, a primary or grade school not far from our house in Kaduna.

I became pregnant again, not too long after we arrived at Kaduna, and gave birth in 1960 to our second child—a son—whom we named Christopher after his father. But we did not stay very long in Kaduna. My husband's skills and work ethic impressed his superiors, and on their recommendation the Nigerian government sent him to work at another training center for students interested in learning arts and crafts. We were transferred again within the Northern Region, this time to Gombe, about 325 miles from Kaduna.

Far from developed at this time, Gombe was home to many of the Hausa and Fulani people, two of the more than 300 ethnic groups in Nigeria. Because I had previously worked in the Western Region, I was familiar with many of the customs and the basic rudiments of both languages, which enabled me to get a job at a primary school for Hausa and Fulani children. Being able to speak the Hausa language fluently also made it easier for me to develop great rapport with my students and their parents.

We had two more children while living in Gombe – Francis and Maryann – and I worked very hard at redefining the concept of a working mother. Most Nigerian women stayed home with their children, but I was determined to continue teaching, and providing support for my family, a role I most desired and cherished.

My father did not immediately remarry after my mother's death, but later our family urged him to remarry, even though his health was in decline. He eventually married a young woman, Cecilia, with whom he had two more children, one of whom died in infancy. The surviving child, however, was still quite young when my father died on November 17, 1965.

During one of our family vacations to our home village, I managed to convince the parents of three of my young cousins, whose ages ranged between 7 and 10, to let the children live with us. In exchange for agreeing to put them through school, these three young girls would assist Cyril with the housework, laundry, and provide child care for my little children when I was at work.

Based on this arrangement, my young cousins and our houseboy went to school in shifts. One of the girls and Cyril attended the morning session at the school, returning home with me afterwards, while the other two girls attended school in the afternoon. For my cousins, this was an opportunity of a lifetime, receiving an education far beyond what was possible in our own village, and beyond what was possible for the majority of rural Nigerian girls at that time.

*  *  *  *  *

One day, while I was at work, an elderly colleague took one look at me during the lunch break and began laughing aloud.

"The snake done bite you again, Angie?" she said in broken English and loud enough for all of my fellow teachers to hear.

I had no idea what she was talking about, but I was sure I had never been bitten by a snake. I was deathly afraid of reptiles, and ran as fast as I could every time I saw one. As the other teachers joined in the teasing, I realized my colleague was making a joke, but I still had no clue what she was joking about.

The mystery was solved on my way home from school when I ran into my next door neighbor, who was also a teacher at my school. She approached me, placing her hands on my shoulders, and looking me in the eye.

"Mama Winnie?"

Customarily, women did not usually address one another by their first names, but by adding "Mama" to the first name of their eldest child.

"Yes, Mama Edith?"

"They are saying at school that you are pregnant. The snake has bitten you again, eh?"

In my naiveté, I wondered how I could possibly be pregnant since it had only been four months since Maryann's birth. I did not have any symptoms, and neither my husband nor I knew. How did the teachers know then? In spite of our education, Christopher and I were not quite versed in these matters at this time in our marriage.

This was distressing news to me, and I cried all the way home, thinking about my previous difficult experiences during childbirth. I almost died giving birth to my son, Francis, and had to travel for two days to get to a hospital in Jos, a large metropolitan city in the Northern Region, to deliver Maryann. Now, I wondered what my husband and I would do about this fifth baby.

I remained anxious after I got home until I was able to share this distressing news with my husband. But rather than be upset, Christopher was surprisingly happy, even though he was concerned about my condition.

"Don't worry, Angelina," Christopher said, embracing me. "You and I are going to carry this pregnancy together. God definitely has a plan for us and He will see us through."

What a relief to my soul! Christopher was a man of great faith and trust in God. His words gave me the peace of mind that I craved and calmed my racing heart. The next day, my husband went to seek advice from the local doctor who prescribed prenatal vitamins and other nourishment that I would need for a healthy pregnancy.

Even though I was entitled to begin my fully paid three months of maternity leave as early as six weeks before the birth of my baby, I felt so healthy that I worked until my baby girl was born. We named her Margaret Mary, but I gave her the nickname Maudlyne, which means blossoms. I named her for my friend Nelly Maudlyne Okafor, who made my wedding gown. With Maudlyne's birth, we were now a family of seven.

＊ ＊ ＊ ＊ ＊

Christopher and I discussed the possibility of my undergoing an operation that would prevent me from becoming pregnant again. There was a new Pakistani doctor in Gombe, who had reportedly performed tubal ligation surgery, but the procedure was discussed only in whispers. We made an appointment to see the doctor, not knowing at the time that tubal ligation was a violation of our Catholic teachings.

Four days before my scheduled appointment with the doctor, the entire town seemed to be in an uproar, and people were literally screaming on the streets. Several women on whom the new doctor had performed the procedure had died on the operating table. Needless to say, Christopher and I viewed the deaths as a sign from God.

"You are not going to have that operation," he said to me. "I don't care if you have 10 children. God will make a way for us to care for them."

We never discussed pregnancy or tubal ligation again. Instead, we focused our efforts on raising our five children and keeping them safe and healthy.

| Chapter 8 | # FLEEING FROM NORTHERN NIGERIA |
|-----------|--------------------------------|

Nigeria was quick to follow in Ghana's footsteps by gaining political independence in 1960. Although Christopher and I were not personally involved in the politics of the newly-independent Nigeria, its effects changed everything for our family. Not too long after the fireworks celebrating independence had been extinguished, the fledgling Nigerian government was rocked by regional factionalism, military coups and assassinations. The country had been degenerating politically since independence. By early 1965, sporadic violence had erupted throughout the country, and according to the daily media reports, the targets of this violence very often were Igbos—our people, our tribe.

On January 15, 1966, there was a military coup in Nigeria against the federal government. The coup was led by Major Chukwuma Kaduna Nzeogwu, along with a group of fellow majors who were predominantly of eastern origin. This coup resulted in the assassination of some key players in the federal government of Nigeria, including the Prime Minister, a federal minister, two regional premiers, as well as numerous Army officers and many civilians.

The coup had succeeded in the northern region where the majority of those assassinated were northerners, and it would soon be observed that it hardly took place in the east and other regions. Major General Aguiyi Ironsi, an Igbo, had been marked for elimination, but he managed to elude the coup plotters, out maneuvering and seizing power from them, and arresting them. Because of the unsavoury state of affairs in the country, the young officers were initially hailed by a great number of the Nigerian populace, but soon the sentiment would shift and the coup would be viewed as an Igbo conspiracy. This quickly degenerated into a crisis of confidence, heightening ethnic sentiments and divisive ideas. It was not long before the rumor spread that the coup was a grand design by the Igbo to eliminate their presumed obstacles and make way for Igbo domination of the whole country. Faced with this accusation, the Igbos had no credible explanation for the sectional method adopted by the coup plotters. Although only a handful of Igbo officers carried out the coup, the Igbos as a group were being condemned and looked upon as potential enemies based on what these few officers had done.

One is inclined to wonder whether that was a fair assessment of the situation. It was mainly the Igbos who had been moving around the country, particularly during the 1940s and 1950s, to fill vacant positions as educators, clerks, bank tellers, government officials, engineers, train drivers, factory workers, and so on.

\* \* \* \* \*

Not knowing for sure where the violence and factionalism would lead, Christopher and I began making tentative plans to eventually leave the north and return to our home village in the Eastern Region. In 1965, when school was over for the long summer holidays, Christopher traveled to Okwu Nguru, where he organized workers to begin work on laying the foundation of a house for our family. Upon his return from our home village, Christopher sat me down to discuss our future and the plans he envisioned we should follow.

"You know, my teaching certificate and the experience I have acquired working in the Northern Region will not count towards a higher position or a possible promotion for me when we return to the Eastern Region," he said. "I will need more education in order to get a better job. Perhaps, now is the best time for me to finish my college degree."

Christopher held an "Inter BSC," the equivalent of an Associate degree, having already completed half of the coursework toward a college degree through correspondence with a university in the United Kingdom. Still, he would need better credentials to get a good position in the civil service when we moved back to the East.

Even after independence, the Igbo people were still reputed to be Nigeria's most highly educated. Moving back to the east to seek employment meant Christopher would have to compete with the many other highly qualified people for any available position.

"You are very right," I said. "I will do my part, trusting that God will strengthen and guide me."

This decision meant my husband would have to leave the country to complete his university studies. I recall feeling quite sad that Christopher would soon be leaving our family to go to school, but I was also happy to realize that attending a university in another African country or studying overseas would give him a much better chance of competing for jobs in the Eastern Region. Leaving Nigeria to go to school was a bittersweet opportunity for Christopher, but it was the first step in the direction leading to long-term stability for our family.

"Where will you go?" I asked.

"I have already been accepted at Fourah Bay University in Sierra Leone," he proudly replied.

Although Fourah Bay was located in West Africa, about three days travel from Gombe, I was relieved that at least Christopher was not planning to go overseas without me!

"How much time do you think you will need to finish at Fourah Bay?" I asked.

"I will study very hard, Angelina. I think I can finish my degree in about two years at the most, and will come home during summer holidays to be with you and the children and finish building our house in Okwu Nguru," he replied.

I nodded in agreement, swallowing back any objections that might stand in the way of this plan that would benefit our family immensely. I was not worried about being alone with the children, as I would be able to find the help to care for them. But because Gombe was in a remote part of the Northern Region, the increasing number of reports of ethnic strife going on throughout the country had many Igbos on edge. Thankfully, Christopher had been thinking about this, and used his government connections to plan ahead for our family.

"I found out that there is an all-girls' teacher training college at Zonkwa, near where we used to live, on the North East railroad," my husband said. "I have already applied on your behalf and you have been accepted. You and the children will be moving to Zonkwa. The principal and other administrators with whom I spoke sounded very excited at the prospect of having someone as qualified as you on their staff," he added.

Within weeks, we had packed and loaded a truck and were on our way to Zonkwa, more than 200 miles west. The school was still in the Northern Region, but it was situated near a train station that could take us directly to the Eastern Region in the event we needed to quickly leave. It felt surreal to be making plans based on the possibility of being attacked because we were Igbo, but that was the reality of the Nigeria Christopher and I painfully watched unfolding before our very eyes.

* * * * *

On arrival, the nuns warmly welcomed us to Zonkwa, a small agricultural community. Mother Superior told me I would be the only married teacher living in the convent, and the first ever to live there with children. I was one of only three Igbo teachers working at the all girls' school, and the rest of the teachers were either Irish or English.

Christopher made sure we were settled at the convent before he left the country in December of 1965. Our houseboy Cyril soon left in order to get married, and was more than thrilled because of the support we had given him to start his new life. Cyril's departure meant I had to find new ways to maintain my family's equilibrium. My three young cousins tackled the household chores, and I taught them domestic science ethics: cooking, baking, cleaning, and laundry skills.

Without Christopher's salary, I also had to devise other means of bringing in more revenue. I thought about my grandmother and my mother, both of whom were successful tradeswomen, and knew immediately what I must do. I would put to use the advanced training I received at the Singer Sewing Institute just before I married Christopher. Although I was already a skilled seamstress, just by observing my mother, the training at the institute enabled me to fine-tune my skills. I suddenly realized that my decision to take that course was a life saver. Like my mother and grandmother, I had acquired the skills I would need to amply support my family.

To supplement my salary from my teaching, I began making uniforms for students, and with the assistance of my young cousins, I also baked *chin-chin* and *puff-puffs*. I sold the hot delicacies every morning to the always-hungry students, and my products were widely reputed to be the best in the area. Whenever I had the opportunity, I traveled to Jos to purchase items I thought the students would like, and made extra money reselling those goods.

It was tough hustling to stay afloat, but it paid off. In hindsight, I am astonished by my apparent success as the sole breadwinner for my family, supporting myself and 10 people—Christopher, his widowed mother Janet, our five children, and my three young cousins. Thinking about it now, I can see the hand of God in all of my endeavors to keep my family secure in Christopher's absence, so much so that I was even able to save money at the Barclays Bank.

* * * * *

Meanwhile the anti-Igbo sentiment and political turmoil following the coup continued to simmer, unleashing a tyrannical wave of brutality against Igbos, particularly in the Northern Region. The daily media reports about the massacres of tens of thousands of Igbos, detailing how they were beaten, stabbed or cut to pieces with machetes horrified everyone. There were reports that people had been mangled, maimed and burned beyond recognition, and some had even been buried alive. Every Igbo became a target - men, women and children, people young and old.

This dire development triggered the first mass exodus of the Igbos to the Eastern Region within days of the initial massacre. Because of their great number, there were not enough trucks and trains to take them home to the East—some even set off on foot—all in an effort to escape the growing hostilities. The government issued decrees ordering an end to the attacks, but that did not abate the killings.

I began packing some of my family's belongings as a precautionary measure, but in my heart, I did not believe the unrest would ever reach the remote countryside where we were now living. I prayed daily at morning mass for God's protection, while doing my best to see that my family maintained as normal a life as possible.

*  *  *  *  *

Every week, I would ride my moped to the neighborhood market to purchase cooking supplies. I always greeted the local tradesmen, most of whom were Hausa, in their native language. My ability to communicate in many of the languages and dialects of other Nigerian tribes endeared me to many people in Zonkwa. The Hausa tradesmen referred to me as "Madam Keke," meaning "Madam Bicycle," as they regarded my moped as a bike. I was to learn later that riding my moped was viewed by the men as violating the customary Muslim tradition that forbade women from riding a bike, claiming it would be difficult for them to maintain discretion on a bike while wearing a dress.

In May of 1966, the principal of my school left Nigeria to return to the United Kingdom for an extended vacation. I had been recently promoted to the position of vice principal, so she left me in charge. Shortly after my promotion, I rode my moped to the market, and noticed that there were not as many Hausa tradesman as there used to be. I instinctively knew something was wrong, based on the persistent rumors of attacks on Igbos in other parts of the Northern Region, and I was almost certain that the nearly-empty marketplace was a sign of impending trouble.

My concern was confirmed within hours of my return to the school premises. The priest in charge of the rectory made an unannounced visit to the convent, urging me and the other two Igbo teachers to leave everything behind and head straight to the station to catch the 8:00 p.m. train to Enugu, an Igbo city in the Eastern Region. He told me that a local man had confided in him that his next-door Hausa neighbors were plotting to kill all the Igbos in Zonkwa that very night, and that the Hausas would begin arriving in droves by train at 9:00 p.m. from Kaduna, which was only one stop away. It was then close to 7:00 p.m.

With eight young children, I knew we would never be able to walk the mile from the convent to the station in time to catch the train. Thankfully, the priest had already enlisted the assistance of a local doctor from South Africa, who loaded us onto a truck and drove us to the station.

I was unprepared for the scene that awaited us on arrival. The station was teeming with hundreds of adults and children, all nervously chattering simultaneously, and determined to get aboard the next train. They were nervously discussing the reports that bands of marauding Hausas would arrive at the same station in a little more than an hour. To stay alive, we would all have to somehow board the 8:00 p.m. train. I began to pray, my only recourse at difficult times, especially during times like these.

The pushing and shoving commenced as soon as the train pulled into the station. It was already packed with fleeing Easterners from Lagos and other towns and villages along the rail line, but that did not stop everyone on the Zonkwa platform from fighting to board the train. As the pushing and shoving intensified, God placed an angel in my path. The stationmaster walked over to me and began helping me and my children to get in the train by passing the six oldest children through the train's windows. With the youngest child strapped on my back, I gripped the hand of the second youngest and pushed through the crowd until we were all safely on board.

Inside the train, I continued to yell the names of my oldest children: "Winifred! Christopher! Francis!" In spite of the clamor, they were able to hear my voice and followed it to get to where I was on the train. I wanted all of us to stay together, and we sat on top of the piles of luggage in the cramped, smothering quarters of the train.

I would learn later that the Hausas entered the Zonkwa convent at 2:00 a.m. looking for "Madame Keke" and the other Igbos. I would hear stories about the massacre and rape of Igbo nurses who had been away in Kaduna where they were taking some exams and were returning to the convent after my family and the other two Igbo teachers had been evacuated. A few of the nurses did escape to the maternity hospital next to the college where they were lucky to be sheltered by co-workers. But I was not able to know the fate of the Igbo students at the school, or that of the stationmaster who helped me and my family. I simply prayed and hoped that God had saved them, too.

* * * * *

The trip was treacherously long for most of the people aboard the train, particularly for those who had boarded first in Lagos. The British only built train tracks from the south of Nigeria, where the seaports and oil refineries were located, to the arid north where they preferred to live. To travel west or east required first heading to the north-south tracks and then catching a truck going east or west.

Because there had been no east-west tracks, and violence against Igbos had made it unsafe to travel across the country by truck, the Igbos who boarded the train in Lagos had to travel more than twice the distance, about 563 miles north to Zonkwa, plus an additional 350 miles south to Enugu. They had already been aboard the train for more than two days when my family came on board for the last leg of the journey.

There was no leg room anywhere on the train, and pregnant women and the elderly suffered with swollen limbs. Children on board the train were crying because they were hungry; the elders were moaning, and there were nervous screams and a general feeling of despair all around. The train was stuffy and as hot as an oven. At every station, bodies of people who had died as a result of the overcrowding were tossed from the train, eliciting from the weary passengers sorrowful, mournful wails.

I regretted not bringing food for my children, knowing they must be hungry. In our rush to leave the convent, I only had the presence of mind to grab my "*isusu*" funds. The *isusu* is an Igbo tradition whereby a group of people, usually colleagues or close friends, would pledge to contribute a set amount of money every month, and the total amount would be collected by one member of that group at the end of the month, usually in an agreed order. This process would be repeated until everyone in the group had collected. We had this arrangement in my school and each of my fellow teachers contributed Ten British Pounds Sterling every month toward the *isusu*. I elected to be the last to collect, and this coincided with the month we were fleeing from the North. The payout was handed to me on the day before we left Zonkwa. As we departed from the convent, I secured the cash in my waist wrapper, thinking I would have time to purchase bread and sardines for my children on the way to the train station. But there had been no time to stop and shop. Thankfully, food vendors were milling around at the train station. Afraid to lose their seats, the passengers purchased snacks and food by sticking their arms out of the window, and waving the cash.

As the train rolled across the countryside, I suddenly had a frightening thought about Christopher, who had no idea what was happening to our family. What if he returned to Zonkwa looking for us? I quickly banished that thought, preferring instead to focus on the immediate concerns. We were headed to the Eastern Region where we had family, but no home for the nine of us. It would be my sole responsibility to put food on the table for my children, find them shelter, and ensure their safety. Realizing that fear was not an option, I hung on to the Lord in trust and hope.

# Chapter 9 | BEGINNING LIFE ANEW IN THE EASTERN REGION

Like all of the Igbos on that train who had left everything behind, we were starting our lives all over again as we disembarked in Enugu. Thankfully, my brother James lived there, and we would be able to stay with him for a few days before tackling the last leg of our journey to Okwu Nguru. As exhausted as we all were, my children and I walked from the train station to my brother's home. James immediately made room in his house for my family, and the eight children and I crowded into the one bedroom and slept on straw mats on the floor. Compared to the situation in the train, we could not complain about this arrangement, which seemed to be paradise for all of us!

Enugu would soon be teeming with Igbo people returning home. They were everywhere - on the streets, in the markets and in the churches. The Igbos had once lived all over Nigeria as legitimate citizens of our nation, contributing immeasurably to the development of our country. Now, we were being treated as outcasts, banished strictly to our home region. Many historians and anthropologists would later refer to us as the "Jews of West Africa" because of the apparent similarities between the expulsion and massacre of the Igbos and the persecution and acts of genocide against the Jews in Germany.

We had become refugees in our homeland, and there were little or no assurances of welcome. Some of us would be subjected to mockery in our home villages because we had come home with nothing, and literally had to beg for accommodation, and sometimes even food.

"We thought you made a lot of money over there," a relative would indignantly charge. "We thought you were living the luxury life. Now you are back with no place to stay? Were you too good to think about building a house?"

This situation saddened me because many of the mockers had been beneficiaries of the refugees' so-called luxury life in other regions. But were we living a life of luxury? Every Igbo family I knew not only supported their immediate family, but also sent money home to support family members in the Eastern Region. The mockers seemed to have forgotten all of that sacrifice.

My children and I ended up staying at James's home for one week, arriving on Sunday and departing for Okwu Nguru the following Saturday. From Enugu, my family and I traveled almost 80 miles south to Umuahia by train. To get to our village six miles away, we had to catch a truck, sitting on wooden benches in its open back. Finally, the driver dropped my weary family off at the edge of Christopher's home village.

The children and I moved in with Christopher's uncle Sylvanus, the brother of his deceased father. Once again, we crowded into a single room. About a week after returning to Okwu, my young cousins returned to their own families, who were greatly relieved that we made it safely back to the

Eastern Region. I also mailed a letter to Christopher to let him know that we had returned to the village and that we were safe.

While we lived with my husband's uncle, I was able to resume work on the house Christopher had begun to build for us. The *"isusu"* funds I had secured in my waist wrapper proved to be my salvation. Not only was I able to continue to feed my family, I was also able to resume work on our own house, buying the bricks, nails, zinc for the roof, asbestos for the ceiling, wood for the frame, and paying for labor.

Gradually, my *"isusu"* funds were used up, but I was not worried. I traveled by truck to Umuahia to a branch of Barclays Bank where I had saved the surplus from my teaching, sewing, and selling of *puff-puffs* and *chin-chin* to school children in Zonkwa. During the truck ride, I chuckled as I thought about my grandmother, the tobacco tradeswoman with whom I lived the first five years of my life. She knew nothing about modern banks, but her own bank had been a room in her house which she filled with piles of cowrie shells, the currency of her day. At the end of every day, my grandmother would add to that pile, keeping only a small reserve for food and household needs. Many years later, I would follow in her footsteps by saving my money at a real bank, and being in a position to cater to the needs of my family, particularly in a time of crisis and despair. Today, I pay tribute to my grandmother for bequeathing to me an enduring legacy and for her clarity of vision which had evidently rubbed off on me.

* * * * *

Christopher was able to make his way to us in Okwu Nguru from Fourah Bay in Sierra Leone during the summer holidays in June of 1966. The construction of our house was well underway, but our family was still living with his uncle. Within days of Christopher's arrival home, we heard on the BBC World News Service that Major Gen. Aguyi Ironsi, the Supreme Commander of the Nigerian Armed Forces, had been assassinated in a countercoup, and scores of Igbo military officers based in the Northern Region had also been killed.

At the same time, some senior military officers from the Northern Region, based in the capital city of Lagos, seized control of the country and established a new federal government under the leadership of Lt. Col. Yakubu Gowon. The BBC reported that Gowon had ordered an immediate ceasefire and a halt to the attacks on the Igbos, but fear had been planted in our people's hearts and no one thought the calm would last.

Hearing reports about the cessation of hostilities against the Igbos, Christopher immediately began planning to return to Zonkwa to retrieve our belongings. But before he could execute his plan, however, he had to spend an additional few days convincing his mother Janet that it was safe for him to travel by truck and train to the Northern Region and back. Christopher had planned that upon his arrival in Zonkwa, he would transport our belongings to the freight train station, and then board a passenger train and return home within three days. Despite my own reservations, Christopher managed to convince me that his plan would work. After all, he had spent his entire career teaching in the Northern Region and spoke Hausa and Fulani flawlessly.

Finally, Janet relented when she learned I had already packed most of our belongings in the house at Zonkwa, but still Christopher's daring plan was cause for great alarm.

During the days that Christopher was away, her mood was mournful, and she angrily said to me that she would blame me if anything happened to her only son. This made me pray harder to St. Jude, fervently imploring him to pray for my husband's protection, constantly reminding God that my children needed their father, and Janet her son. Thankfully, my prayers were answered, as Christopher safely and miraculously returned home to Okwu within the timeframe he had projected.

After his trip to Zonkwa, Christopher spent the rest of July and part of August with our family. He worked on the house and played with and comforted our children. Whenever we had the opportunity to talk, my husband reassured me that once he completed school, we would be together, and we would be able to create a secure and prosperous future for our family, which still included our original plan of moving overseas.

* * * * *

At the end of the summer, Christopher had to face danger again. In order to catch a flight back to Sierra Leone and return to Fourah Bay, my husband would have to travel through western Nigeria by truck and then south to Lagos by train. I had no way of knowing at the time that the borders of our country would soon be closed, and that the Eastern Region of Nigeria would be slowly cut off from the rest of the country and the world. I had no way of knowing that my mind would soon be burdened with thoughts of survival for my family and the entire Igbo race.

I would not know my husband's fate for more than two years. Besides, neither Christopher nor I knew when he departed that I was pregnant with our sixth child.

# PART II

*Africa had won its first round for self-determination in gaining independence from colonialism. Now it was facing a second: the demand of Africa's many ethnic groups to shape their own destinies without being bound to the colonial-imposed concept of "territorial integrity."*

*In Biafra's case, the war was more than defense of principle; it involved the question of the survival of one of Africa's most industrious peoples (the Igbos), who had been in the forefront of the drive for freedom from British rule.....*

*Even before the fighting began, it was evident that the East's secession was neither the dream nor the act of a single man. And when secession did come, millions of Easterners were clearly resolved to die in the defense of their new homeland, no matter what Lagos said about this being "Ojukwu's war..."*

*If Biafrans had their backs to the wall, this fact had hardly touched their morale. Never had an African people appeared more united."*

*New York Times*
March 31, 1968

## Biafra

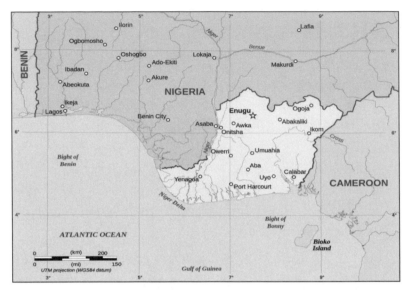

*Home to 13 million people, primarily Igbo, in a geographic area the size of South Carolina. Nigeria's most bountiful natural resource — the world's purest oil — is located within the boundaries of Biafra.*

| Chapter 10 | **EFFORTS TO KEEP NIGERIA ONE** |

Lt. Col. Gowon abolished the unification decree, the fragile thread holding the country together, and instituted what he called the federal government system in September of 1966. This action set off alarms in both the Western and Eastern Regions, and rumors spread that Gowon, a Christian from the north, was preparing the nation for Northern domination.

The BBC radio remained our source of information regarding the mounting calamity swirling around us. We heard daily reports about the crisis looming around Lt. Col. Odumegwu Ojukwu, the military governor of the Eastern Region. Somehow, he had to figure out a way to make room in our region for the millions of Igbos fleeing massacres and persecution in the north and west. These people would all need food, shelter and clothing, but pandemonium and fear prevailed.

On September 29, 1966, mob violence broke out against tens of thousands of Igbos in the Northern Region, a day that would become known in Nigeria's history as "Black Thursday." Instead of protecting the Igbos, there were reports that the Northern troops actively participated in the attacks. Gowon publicly deplored the violence, but did not offer either condolences or compensation to the victims' families.

In response to media reports that as many as 50,000 Igbo civil servants, shopkeepers and service workers had been slaughtered over a 10 day period, Ojukwu organized for the Igbos to be airlifted back to the our homeland. It was estimated that there were at least 10,000 Hausas living in the Eastern Region during that time, most of them traders, truckers or herdsmen, and Ojukwu equally arranged that they be evacuated so as to guarantee their safety.

The military governor's action triggered a similar reaction by other tribal groups, and suddenly Nigeria was undergoing a massive, cross-country migration of people forced to return to their ancestral lands. Soon there was talk that the nation would be divided along tribal lines.

To stem the growing crisis, Ojukwu sought help from Gowon. The two men were close in age and both had received their military training in the United Kingdom, and had once been friends in the early days of their military careers. Reports of the series of their telephone dialogues spread quickly and, for a while, these conversations were a source of hope that our people would be safe and the ethnic tensions would subside. We were especially happy to hear Gowon's announcement that he had personally halted the execution of several Igbo military officers and made sure they were safely transported back to the East.

In spite of all the assurances, fear was increasingly brewing amongst the Igbo, and they responded to the growing attacks by calling for secession from Nigeria, and the formation of an independent nation state. It is my belief that the secession was actually forced upon the Igbos. We loved our country with all our hearts, and based on that love, we Igbos moved around the length and breadth of Nigeria, and truly set up home and settled wherever we went. We worked hard and invested in the communities in which we lived. The executions and massacres forced us all to rethink our patriotism, and for the first time, I too, began to think of secession as the only way to save our people.

\* \* \* \* \*

Amidst the reports of the violence perpetrated against the Igbos, we the returnees to the Eastern Region faced a huge dilemma. In spite of the major blow to our lives, a semblance of order prevailed: our courts were in operation; the markets remained open; our church services continued without disruption, and our children still went to school. I was determined not to be distracted by the news reports or discouraged because I had not heard from Christopher. Instead, I focused on working to bring some sort of normalcy to my children's lives.

I also knew that I needed to find a regular job, and was soon recruited to teach at Regina Caeli Teacher Training College, a school not far from Okwu Nguru, and situated between the villages of Obeama and Ogwu. After a few weeks of working there, the principal offered me housing on the school campus, and I moved in with my children. Shortly thereafter, I arranged to bring one of my cousins, Angelina, to live with us and attend school, and help me with chores and childcare. Angelina was named after me by a beloved paternal uncle and his wife.

For the first time since leaving Zonkwa, my family finally had room to stretch out and fully relax: we had 3 bedrooms, a kitchen and a living room area to call our own, as well as a

"Boy's Quarters" for domestic workers. I enjoyed teaching everything in the curriculum, such as mathematics, psychology, principles of education, methods of teaching, English, history, and so on. The future teachers were very eager to learn.

In late fall of 1966, there was an international conference that attracted a diverse, cross-section of social, educational and political experts, and brought foreign journalists to the Eastern Region. Some of the journalists visited Regina Caeli, and I was chosen to be interviewed. This afforded me the opportunity to talk about the value of educating young girls, based on my own educational experience, and share the story of how my family barely escaped the attacks at my former school in Zonkwa. The foreigners were moved by all of the harrowing stories they had heard.

Unbeknownst to me, Sister Mary Theodore, the principal of Owerri Girls' Secondary School, Owerri, was listening to the interview, and approached me as soon as the journalists moved on to interview someone else.

"You spoke so eloquently," Sister Mary Theodore said.

"Thank you, Sister," I replied.

"I want you to come teach English at my school."

"But my..."

"You are better qualified to teach at a secondary school than at a teacher training college," the nun insisted. "My girls need teachers like you."

I was indeed thrilled to hear this. My background had amply prepared me to teach at the secondary school level, based on my education at Cornelia Connelly College and St. Theresa's, and I believed it was important for the students to be taught by native teachers. The principal's offer was hard to refuse. I loved being in the classroom, watching the young girls' eyes open wide with wonder as I taught them, and watching them grow in understanding. So I transferred from Regina Caeli to Owerri Girls' Secondary School in January of 1967.

Once again, I was offered housing on campus and happily moved in with my children. In addition to my young cousin Angelina, my sister Theresa's daughter, Uche, came to live with us at Owerri. Uche's parents had also escaped the massacre of Igbos in Lagos, and now sent their daughter to me so that she could go to school. At that time, the school had both morning and afternoon sessions, and my young cousin and niece conveniently attended school and assisted me with childcare.

Every morning at mass, I expressed gratitude to God for the safety and well-being of my family, and implored Him to keep His eye on Christopher as well.

* * * * *

Despite their best efforts, both Ojukwu and Gowon had different visions for the future of Nigeria. Leaders of Ghana's independence movement, recognizing that the stakes were very high for all of Africa, arranged for the two leaders to meet at Aburi, Ghana, in January of 1967. They had hoped to negotiate a plan to end the hostilities and attacks against the Igbos, and propagate Nigerian unity, but that was not to be.

During the two days of meetings, a peace agreement that would become known as the Aburi Accord was negotiated. But when all of the parties returned to Nigeria, efforts to implement the accord failed, and ethnic tensions escalated once again. We from the Eastern Region were forced to recognize that our only option under the circumstance was secession. The Nigerian government's previous threats seemed to imply that a civil war was imminent.

These events scared people like me who had studied the histories of both civil and world wars. But there were others who were ignorant of what war entailed, and so yearned for battle, wishing for it to be declared immediately. Some people thought the war would be like a wrestling contest between two giants, which would be over in a twinkling of an eye, but I knew differently. Still, like everyone else, I waited for the events to unfold, like a pregnant woman awaiting the onset of labor.

* * * * *

My own real labor contractions began while I was in the middle of teaching a math class, and I immediately sent for help through one of my students. The next thing I knew, I was being rushed by car to the maternity hospital in Awaka, a village about four miles from Owerri. While I was in the delivery room giving birth to our fourth daughter, Rosemary, on May 10, 1967, the hospital was agog with rumors that the Nigerian Army had overrun Owerri. Instinctively, I knew I had to hurry up with the delivery of the baby and get my children out of the city and to safety.

Within one hour of giving birth, the owner of the maternity hospital, Mrs. Matilda Nwachukwu, and my colleagues from work who had accompanied me to the hospital, helped to get me and my newborn baby out of the premises. We took a truck back to Owerri Girls' Secondary School, and to my surprise, my husband's friend, Stephen Ejiogu, had been waiting for me at my house in Owerri. With no time to waste, Stephen packed up everybody in his van, and raced us back to Okwu Nguru. It was a treacherous trip that took several hours, even though the distance was only about 40 miles.

My own car was driven to the village by a man that accompanied Stephen. I had bought this small car, a Morris Minor, from my principal, Sr. Mary Theodore, on condition that I would pay for it by monthly installments, which she would be deducting from my salary. The car had been left in her care by one of her expatriate teachers who had left following the Nigerian government's announcement urging all foreigners to leave Biafra. I had made only a few payments on the car when we had to flee from Owerri to the village, and shortly afterwards, the principal herself left for Ireland. So I literally got that car for free.

After fleeing Owerri, we went back to live with Christopher's Uncle Sylvanus. My niece Uche returned home to her parents, but my cousin, Angelina, remained with me. Once again, eight of us had to crowd into a small room in Sylvanus' home. Christopher's uncle Sylvanus was a very generous man, and had equally accommodated other extended family members. Not surprisingly, the cramped living conditions often triggered fights between my children and the other relatives' children.

These incessant fights spurred me to double my efforts in ensuring that work on the building of our own home was expedited. When the walls were still wet with fresh paint and the wood doors and windows had barely been installed, I decided it was time for us to move in, and my mother-in-law Janet moved in with us. We would finish work on the interior of the house as resources became available.

Being unemployed once more, and in an effort to adequately cater to my family's needs and find other means of adding to my savings at the Barclays Bank, I had to resort to petty trading. This was when my little car became a treasure. I regularly drove to Oguta and Egbema to buy dried fish, garri, and fresh vegetables, items that I later resold at a profit. There was always something to be done, and I did whatever that I needed to do for my family's survival.

At some point, I had to harvest the cassava which I had planted during the farming season, and with the help of my children, I processed the cassava to garri by first cleaning the tubers, grating, drying, and then frying the dried paste as garri. As an educated teacher, I often thought about what led to these tedious and painstaking efforts and how the present circumstances had literally turned me into an illiterate woman selling her wares in the market stall. My one consolation was that the hustling kept me occupied, took my mind from the devastating thoughts of the war, and above all, my profits from these endeavors benefited my family and others around us. I hardly had any dull moments.

Finally, my family had its own home, and I was happy that my children had room to play with one another without getting into a fight.

# Chapter 11 | BIAFRA IS BORN

In a bid to counteract the calls coming from the east for secession, Lt. Col. Yakubu Gowon invoked a nationwide state of emergency on May 27, 1967. At the same time, he promulgated a decree that the nation's four regions would be divided into 12 states. According to the decree, the Eastern Region would comprise three states. Under the proposal, Lt. Col. Odumegwu Ojukwu would remain the military governor of what was then known as the East Central State. But the Igbos would be landlocked and denied access to our historically controlled resources, such as the seaport and the nation's richest oil reserves. The decree came as a shock to the Igbos, but everyone anxiously awaited Ojukwu's reaction and subsequent announcement of how we would tackle the situation.

Looking back, I think the decree aroused the indignation of our people, who had already suffered the loss of thousands, possibly hundreds of thousands of lives. But as the Eastern Region was doing its best to cope with the ongoing refugee crisis, Ojukwu was being bombarded with demands, particularly from the intellectual community, for secession—to form our own nation. These people firmly believed we had the political capital, natural resources, scientific know-how and labor reserves to make it without the federal government. There was talk that our nation would be called the Republic of Biafra, named for the Bight of Biafra, an inlet of the Gulf of Guinea, along the coast of the Eastern Region. And we would be called Biafrans.

The demand was so strong that most felt that secession was imminent. I somehow thought that my family was safe since we did not live close to any of the potential centers of military action.

* * * * *

On May 30, 1967, Ojukwu announced that the eastern region's 300-member Consultative Assembly had given him the mandate to secede. His address to the people of the Eastern Region was broadcast over the radio, and every adult huddled together around the radio to hear his speech. An excerpt from the speech reads thus:

> *Having mandated me to proclaim on your behalf, and in your name, that Eastern Nigeria be a sovereign independent Republic; now, therefore I, Lieutenant Colonel Chukwuemeka Odumegwu-Ojukwu, Military Governor of Eastern Nigeria, by virtue of the authority, and pursuant to the principles recited above, do hereby solemnly proclaim that the territory and region known as and called Eastern Nigeria together with her continental shelf and territorial waters, shall, henceforth, be an independent sovereign state of the name and title of The Republic of Biafra.*

With this, the Igbos took to the streets in Enugu, our newly designated capital, with shouts of "Biafra, now!" Biafra suddenly was a country, an underdeveloped, but oil-rich nation. Historians would later describe it as the Japan, the Israel, the Manchester and the Kuwait of Africa. They would contend that it was the oil, as well as the Igbos ancient tribal traditions of ambition, hard work and commitment to individual success, that made their desire for secession unpopular and untenable to the rest of Nigeria.

Despite the stalemate which the government of Nigeria later acknowledged that it had helped trigger, the secession was publicly portrayed to the rest of Nigeria, and eventually to the world, as having been organized by "Biafran dissidents" and "rebels" intent on robbing the rest of the country of all of its important resources. Following Ojukwu's declaration, Gowon immediately dispatched riot police officers to guard key government facilities, such as the power station and radio transmitter. Roadblocks were set up in Lagos and other major cities, in readiness for apprehending saboteurs.

The tensions were heightened when Chief Awolowo and other Yoruba tribal leaders in the Western Region announced that they, too, would secede from Nigeria. Like the newly formed Biafran government, the Yoruba leaders believed their actions were justified after Gowon had redrawn their borders, removing the much coveted port of Lagos from the boundaries of the Western Region.

*  *  *  *  *

The Nigerian military government announced plans to "re-annex" Biafra, and declared war on July 6, 1967, launching a barrage of artillery against Ogoja, a town in the northeast corner of Biafra. Gowon vowed to the western media that the Nigerian army would wrap up "the quick, surgical operation" within 48 hours. His side had tons of weaponry and air support – MIG fighter jets from the Soviets, which were flown by Egyptian pilots, and munitions from the

British. The Soviets also provided torpedo boats and "technicians" to train the Nigerian forces.

\* \* \* \* \*

Sister Mary Theodore, the nun and principal who had hired me to work at Owerri Girls' Secondary School, left the country as soon as war was declared, but many of the other nuns, in solidarity with us, refused to leave, vowing that they were prepared to die in the Eastern Region with the Biafrans. It would be years before I learned of their fates. Unfortunately, the resolve of the nuns was not enough to keep open the doors of Owerri Girls' Secondary School.

\* \* \* \* \*

The Biafrans' quest for independence and sovereignty would soon defy Lt. Col. Gowon's predictions. Despite being outmatched militarily, the primarily barefoot Biafran soldiers showed they had plenty of grit, forcing Gowon to change his prediction from 48 hours to 10 days. Thirty days into the fighting, the Biafrans struck a major blow to the Nigerian side when they captured the Midwestern Region. This meant that all of Nigeria's oil reserves were now in the hands of the Biafrans. The Nigerian civil war was becoming an epic battle between David and Goliath.

\* \* \* \* \*

Now that I was, once again, out of work, the only money I had to care for my family was my savings at Barclays Bank, and in order to stretch those funds, I once more began to trade. I cautiously traveled to neighboring towns and villages to purchase foodstuffs which I brought back home to Okwu to resell. My business soon began to boom, and in the early days of the war, I was able to feed and support my children, my mother-in-law and myself quite comfortably.

My family experienced a major crisis when Biafra was blockaded by Nigeria and with the support of the British, making it extremely difficult for Biafrans to have access to food and medical supplies, among other basic necessities. In desperation, Nigeria had made starvation a weapon of war! Radio Biafra reported that the Nigerian government's strategy on Biafra was setting new standards for inhumanity. For the first time in modern warfare history, starvation was used as a primary weapon. Historical and media reports estimated that about 1,000 Biafran children died daily of starvation, a number that would grow to 6,000 at the height of the war.

Meanwhile, the escalating humanitarian crisis gave the world a tremendous gift when it gave birth to what would later be known as Doctors without Borders. Medical professionals flew to Biafra from around the world in an effort to arrest the growing number of deaths unleashed by *kwashiorkor*, a disease caused by severe malnutrition. In Biafra, this disease took its greatest toll on children and the elderly. Ultimately, it would be the haunting eyes of dying children that would awaken the rest of the world to what was happening in Biafra, and which would give birth to the modern-day international relief movement.

\* \* \* \* \*

Because of the Nigerian government's economic blockade on Biafra, which included the blocking of communication to other countries, it became extremely difficult to send money to my husband, and I was greatly worried by this new development. Christopher was a student and needed to focus on his studies, not his finances. I prayed about this situation and came to the conclusion that Christopher's priority would be the safety and well-being of our children. After that, I turned over all anxiety about my husband's predicament to God, and trusted that Christopher's needs would somehow be met.

I missed my husband dearly, and so did our children and Christopher's mother. Not being able to continue to receive my husband's letters was painful to me, but I had to focus on keeping the rest of our family alive.

# Photos

Figure 1: Angie's mother, Mrs. Martha Ebere Onwunali Nwachukwu

Figure 2: Angie, prior to meeting Christopher Ihejirika

Figure 3: Christopher's family before he met Angie

Figure 4: Christopher (Right) in his bachelor days

Figure 5: Chris and Angie's wedding at Kafanchan, October 12, 1957

Figure 6: Angie and baby Winifred, their first child

Figure 7: Angie, her principal, and fellow teachers at Teacher Training College, Akwanga, Northern Nigeria, 1965

Figure 8: Jim and Helen Wolter, one of the five couples who helped to make our escape from Biafra a reality

Figure 9: Angie and her children arrive in the United States from Biafra. Picture was taken at the residence of Dean Dietz in Northbrook, Illinois, June 1969

Figure 10: The Ihejirika children – Winifred, Christopher, Francis, MaryAnn and Maudlyne – at Jim and Helen Wolter's residence, Christmas, 1973

Figure 11: Angie and Chris after a party in 1973

Figure 12: The Ihejirika family at their first apartment, 2727 South Commons, South Indiana Ave, Chicago, 1970

Figure 13: Angie and Chris at one of Angie's fashion shows, 1975

Figure 14: Angie's family and friends after MaryAnn's wedding

Figure 15: Winifred, the oldest of the Ihejirika children, as a teenager

Figure 16: Angie and friends at St Jerome Catholic Church, Chicago

Figure 17: Installation of pipe borne water in the Ihejirika compound at Okwu Nguru, Aboh Mbaise, Imo State, Nigeria

Figure 18: Mr. and Mrs. Ihejirika at the baptism of their last child, Valentino, their only child born in the United States

Figure 19: Baptism of Valentino Ihejirika, born February 14, 1971

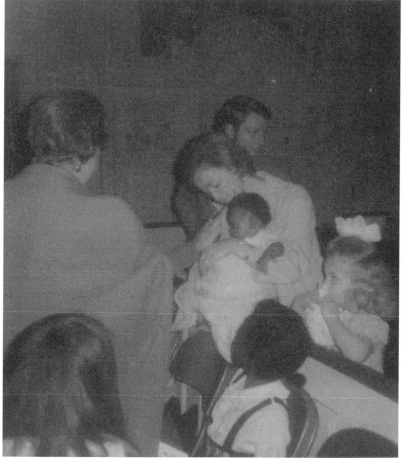

# Chapter 12 | SURVIVING IN BIAFRA

The villages surrounding Owerri, including our village of Okwu Nguru, became targets of the Nigerian air raids while I was recovering from my youngest daughter's birth. Ready to be up and about again, but not wanting to put my children in harm's way, I dug a large bunker next to our house to hide and protect them from the menace of the daily air raids. After packing the children in the bunker, like sardines in a can, I arranged palm fronds on the top of the bunker so as not to give anyone any clues that might endanger the lives of the precious children hiding in the bunker. Janet watched over them from a smaller hole adjacent to the children's bunker.

My greatest concern at this time, besides my children's safety, was food. I sent the three eldest children to the homes of friends who might have extra rations, or to the various Red Cross food stations strewn across nearby villages. These stations were supported and financed by Catholic Charities, an organization based in the United Kingdom and the United States. I had heard the food and medical supplies were smuggled to Biafra via airplanes that landed at night on a makeshift, secret landing strip. The air strip was located in a remote village of Biafra called Uli, in the midst of a thick forest and not too close to a major road.

Once I figured out how to keep my children relatively safe, I resumed my nearly two-mile walk each morning to attend mass at the Holy Rosary Convent on the campus of Regina Caeli. After morning mass, I would return home to make sure my children had breakfast.

I would return later to the convent to join the women who usually came to the school to assemble snack packs for the Biafran soldiers fighting on the front lines. We cracked palm kernels and extracted the nuts, and prepared and dried tapioca from cassava tubers. After the tapioca had been sun dried, we would pack the palm nuts and the tapioca chips together in plastic bags. Since there was hardly any drinking water, the soldiers resorted to cutting tender leaves from the bush in order to extract the juice to soothe their parched throats.

One morning in February of 1968, as the war raged on around Owerri villages, I was returning home from morning mass when the Nigerian air force planes began bombing earlier than usual. I ducked under a mound of cassava stems, and just then a bomb dropped from the sky, landing in front of me on a heap of sand surrounding the cassava stems. I held my breath, momentarily thinking of how to escape from this bomb, and then got up and ran, diving into the bush. I had no idea whether the bomb ever exploded, but it felt surreal to realize that, had it exploded on impact, it would have made a minced meat of me and scattered my body into a million pieces, thereby causing my children to grow up without a mother. No one might have known what happened to me. As soon as the sky was clear again, I got up from the bush and ran all the way home to cradle my children in my arms. That was an experience that would remain with me for the rest of my life.

\* \* \* \* \*

During the spring of 1968, my parish priest asked to speak with me after mass. He wanted to know whether I would help feed refugees in a neighboring village. Of course, I assured him I would gladly assist in that regard, but asked him why he had not considered the hungry people in my own village. Before this encounter with the parish priest, the thought of how to help other refugees whose conditions were definitely worse than those of my family had tortured me, but I could not do much for them until this opportunity presented itself to me. So I did not hesitate to take it.

I told the priest, "If the Red Cross provides the foodstuffs, I will help to feed the refugees and get some assistants, and we will even cook the food in my home." "Are you sure?" The priest asked me. "Father, I am positive and will be extremely happy to be of some help to other people," I answered.

As the priest joyfully agreed to what I had proposed, I immediately saw it as an answer to my prayers. I was already sheltering refugees from the city of Port Harcourt which had recently been attacked and overrun by Nigerian troops. With this new arrangement, I would be in a better position not only to feed my family but also ensure that the refugees in my community had something to eat.

I was not unmindful of the full import of these new developments, and suddenly realized why God had made the completion of our home possible. My home had six spacious rooms, a large parlor, kitchen, toilet, and a veranda, as well as a backyard and a wide open front yard. I readily turned my home into a refugee feeding center, without a doubt in my mind that my life's mission was indeed taking off.

We had plenty of supplies, and all available spaces in my house were used for storage. Catholic Charities provided corned beef, cornmeal, powdered milk, rice, beans, vitamins and clothing. I hired a truck, and it took two to three trips each time to load all the food and supplies from the relief posts and transport them back to my home. I recruited several young, single women in the village to help feed the poor and suffering of my community. These young women were members of the "Mary League," a group that was devoted to honoring the Virgin Mary and her selfless acts. They were elated to have something meaningful to do, and actually derived great pleasure in serving the poor and sick. Just like me, they were relieved to have something to do in place of the drudgery which the war had unleashed on the daily lives of every Biafran.

All the children in the village old enough to carry a small bundle of firewood helped in gathering and bringing their bundles to us to be used for cooking. Members of the "Mary League" cooked the food outside the house in the evening, using cooking pots placed on a tripod and set over an open fire, and returned in the morning to warm the food for serving. They also helped in organizing the sharing of the food to the refugees at the feeding center. Every day, villagers waited in long queues to receive that one rationed meal, and I did my best to ensure no one went away unattended and hungry. Even people from neighboring villages, who had heard about the food center in Okwu, stopped by, but no one, young or old, was ever rejected.

As soon as the feeding time ended, the cooks and volunteers cleaned up while I rushed to the convent to assist the nuns and the women in assembling snack packs for the Biafran soldiers. During one such occasion, Sister Mary Thomas expressed her concern for my well-being. She noted that I seemed to be lost in thought, always gazing into space, as if in a trance.

"What is it?" Sister Mary Thomas asked me. "What is bothering you the most?"

On top of the stress of feeding the refugees at our home, the thought of Christopher's whereabouts and general welfare still haunted me. I thought I was doing a good job of hiding my emotional burden, not wanting my mother-in-law or my children to be unduly anxious. But as soon as Sister Mary Thomas asked, however, my heart was filled with gratitude for the nun's compassionate concern for me and the opportunity to unburden my soul. I took a deep breath, tears flowing uncontrollably down my cheeks, until I managed to control myself again.

"I do not know whether my husband knows we are still alive," I replied. "I have not heard from him in almost two years since he left to return to school in Sierra Leone."

"I imagine that must be quite frightening, but God hears and answers all prayers," the nun replied.

"I have been praying fervently, Sister. I have no doubt at all that God is into this and will be until the end," I murmured quietly through my tears.

I could feel the nun studying my face before she spoke, "I believe I can help you, Angelina," she said.

My eyes relayed my surprise when I heard what she said, but I quickly recomposed myself and simply stared at her. While my heart had refused to believe it was impossible to correspond with Christopher, the current reality of our lives constantly challenged my hopefulness. Looking at Sister Mary Thomas with tearful eyes, I said nothing, even though there was so much to say; my lips stuck together and my legs felt too numb to move.

The nun leaned closer to me and took my hands in hers. "Please go home and write a letter," she said almost in a whisper. "Write your husband's name on the envelope and his address at the university. Place that envelope inside another envelope and bring it back to me."

I stood motionless staring at her.

"You have to do exactly as I have instructed," Sister Mary Thomas firmly said. "Do you understand, Angelina?"

I nodded my head, my eyes welling with emotion, but I was somewhat taken aback by the boldness of the plan the nun was about to unveil. I somehow worried that helping me could brew trouble and further jeopardize the safety of this nun, who had the option to return home to Ireland, but chose to suffer with the Biafrans. I was deeply moved by her compassion, and surprised that despite the haunting faces of refugees surrounding her, she could see my suffering.

"I will address the outer envelope to my sister in Gabon, who is also a nun," she whispered. "I will instruct her to put your letter in another envelope and send it to our brother, the Reverend Father Thomas, in Ireland. From Ireland, the letter will be sent to Fourah Bay University in Sierra Leone. We will pray that the letter will be delivered to your husband."

When the nun disclosed her carefully thought out plan for my benefit, all doubt and pessimism evaporated from my heart, and I believed right away it had been done on faith. I half ran, half skipped all the way home, as I continued to ponder Sister Mary Thomas' daring plan. The more I thought about it as I ran, hopped, and walked to my house, the more I asked God to bless her, as well as all of the nuns who had stayed back in Biafra with her. I implored God to guide, shelter and provide for them until the end of the war. I had not the slightest idea when that would be, but hoped it would be soon, trusting in the infinite love and mercy of God.

I wrote the letter to Christopher that night, meticulously following the nun's instructions. I let him know that the children, his mother and I were now living in our own house, whose foundation he had laid. I narrated to him how our lives had changed since the war, but assured him we were doing just fine, in spite of the circumstances. I wrote that I was praying for the day we would be reunited, and hoping it would be soon.

The next day at morning mass, I gave Sister Mary Thomas the letter.

"God bless you," she told me, patting my hands. "We will pray."

"Thank you, Sister," I replied. "I will be praying, too."

Much as I was hopeful, I still was not sure whether the plan Sister Mary Thomas had outlined would work, even though it was the first glimmer of hope that I had felt since the war started. Now that the countdown to the realization of my miracle had started, I prayed fervently every night that God would bless and protect every hand that would touch and pass along that letter until it got to Christopher. As I prayed, I imagined my letter being delivered into Christopher's eagerly awaiting hands.

As I would learn later, the only news Christopher ever heard about Biafra were stories of doom and unimaginable hardship, like the prospect of total annihilation. He perennially heard reports about the starving children of Biafra who were dying of kwashiorkor, and the daily air raids and bombings masterminded by the Nigerian Air Force. Knowing I did not have a job, he worried ceaselessly about the safety and wellbeing of our family, but it would be dangerous for him to attempt to return to Biafra through Nigeria in the midst of the turmoil.

# Chapter 13 | TAKING CHARGE OF THE RELIEF CENTER FOR REFUGEES

Every day we were confronted with difficult challenges at the refugee camps throughout Biafra, challenges that completely overwhelmed us: overcrowding, insufficient food and medical supplies, serious water shortage, and so on. I worked very hard with the Mary League to maintain continuity for the refugees who came to my house for their daily rations, mainly women and children, and we fed hundreds every single day without incident. But as soon as I had everything running smoothly, a group of men, who paraded themselves as village elders, conspired to hijack the feeding program from me.

I immediately sensed that the elders' quest for power and control could undermine and disrupt our well laid out routine of feeding the hungry daily. I knew for sure that a lack of transparency in the handling of the feeding program could result in Catholic Charities cutting off our quota of relief foodstuffs, thereby inflicting untold hardships on our refugees, as had happened to some refugees at other camps. Although my Igbo traditions required me to defer to the elders, the war-borne crisis had made it imperative that I stand firm. So I refused to hand over control of the program to the men or distribute any of the relief supplies according to their stipulations.

My stance on this matter sent shock waves throughout the entire village, suddenly thrusting me to the fore and making me the center of attention, albeit in a questionable way. No one defied the elders, let alone a woman. Soon, meetings were being convened to discuss the matter, and this compelled the community to take sides. The elders accused me of being "too wise for a woman," and chastised me for not deferring to the men. They held nightly meetings in a bid to take the food center from me, but I found my strength in the loyalty of my supporters. They established an informal security network to protect my home, which housed the relief supplies. While all of this was going on, I had the privilege of enjoying the support of an elder of note, Chief Festus Ogujiuba, who defended me vehemently. A well-educated and trained teacher, he was much respected in the village community.

Traditionally, all disputes in the village were handled at a public meeting, similar to a court hearing. A respected elder would usually preside as judge and the rest of the group, about four or five men of sound judgement, would listen to the testimony of all of the feuding parties. Then the men, much like a jury, would deliberate on the hearings and announce their decision, and their decision was binding. In my case, I thought it would be impossible for the elders to be fair because I was a woman, but I was wrong. To my amazement, my most vocal supporters came to my rescue. They insisted that the elders constitute an impartial panel of villagers to hear the case and make the final ruling, and they agreed.

On the appointed day, the local church was packed full for the hearing, teeming with villagers and refugees who would ultimately be affected should the food center be mismanaged. As soon as everyone had settled down, one of the chiefs on the panel called me up to explain to them how I came to be in charge of the administration of the food center.

I stood up before the assembly and narrated how a priest in another village had asked me to help the sick and hungry in the community he was serving. I explained to the people how I convinced the priest that our village also had many, if not more, hungry men, women and children, who needed to be fed. Continuing, I narrated how the priest had asked me if I could effectively organize the feeding of the people of our village, and I responded in the affirmative: 'Yes, definitely!' Satisfied with my answer, the priest asked me to follow him to his parish in Amaohuru Nguru village, the headquarters of the Catholic Charities, where the relief materials had been stored. I immediately borrowed a car and drove there to collect the items, and recruited the Mary League to help me with the cooking and serving of the food.

Following my presentation, my supporters nosily hailed me and affirmed the authenticity of my story, and I sat down. The next person to speak after me was my elder brother James. Even though I had not solicited his help, he had somehow heard about the problem, and had traveled more than 80 miles to Okwu from Enugu to add his voice to mine in solidarity. Being a well-known politician, most people in the assembly knew my brother James, but his passionate and eloquent speech left many thinking he was a lawyer as well. My brother methodically and effectively dismantled the very bricks that held the elders' conspiracy together, and unflinchingly supported my stand.

The panel of villagers, obviously satisfied with both my testimony and James's speech, unanimously ruled that I remain in charge of the food program at my home, without further disruption by the elders. The verdict caused the entire church to erupt in cheers and applause, and as we left the church grounds, I took a quick glance at the warring elders and the disgust on their faces was undisguised. They had been certain they would win.

Not surprisingly, my detractors, despite the ruling against them, refused to back down. Intent on seeing me fall on my face, they sent an undercover agent in an attempt to coax me into selling some of the food items that Catholic Charities had donated to the refugees. Could these people not see the suffering caused by the raging war? Did they not notice the children's swollen bellies and the elderly women's drooping eyes? How could they dare to think that I would make money from the refugee program or exploit the indigent people of the village that I had been helping? They knew I had been nurtured in convents most of my life; they had seen me walking to morning mass day after day, even in the midst of the non-stop menace of the air raids. They had watched me and the Mary League work all hours of the day and night to prepare and serve food to the most vulnerable and needy. How could they also think I would steal?

"There is no food for sale here, my brother," I told the undercover agent. "But if you are hungry, I would advise you to go to the feeding center at Okpuruokwe any morning and you will be served."

I thought that having passed that test my detractors would leave me alone, but they did not. They continued to scheme to get me taken off the food program, and spread the laughable rumor that educated women were headstrong and must be avoided like a plague.

As I ruminated over the recent events, I finally came to the realization that it was my unshakeable faith in God and my resolve to help the needy that ultimately ensured that my actions at the food program be above reproach, and gave me the impetus to rise above pettiness and suppress my indignation without disrespecting the elders.

One early morning, hours before dawn, I was awakened by a knock at my door, and upon opening it, one of my in-laws, Stephen, the father of my young cousin, Angelina, was standing before me, and I let him in.

Stephen then said, "A group of those elders, not knowing that we were related, had asked me to join in their efforts to subdue you 'one way or the other.' I told them I would get back to them, and that's why I'm here to alert you. You must be very careful, Madame."

"Thank you, my in-law, but I have nothing to fear. I trust God will continue to protect me and the refugee feeding center," I replied.

* * * * *

There was so much hunger and desolation all over Biafra that the focus of the BBC reports began to shift from the battlefront to the fate of the Biafran people. Foreign journalists were dumbstruck by the growing humanitarian crises resulting from the Nigerian government's blockade of Biafra. They had witnessed the crises first hand when they were finally allowed to enter the fledgling Republic of Biafra. The photographs and documentaries of crying children with bloated bellies, looking like scare crows, had shaken awake the people of the West, particularly those of the United Kingdom and the United States. From the *Daily Mirror* to *Time Magazine*, the children's plight begged the world to pay attention.

Already straddled with protests against the Vietnam War, several college campuses and urban centers around the United States soon erupted in demonstrations in support of the starving children of Biafra. The relief efforts masterminded by the International Red Cross and Catholic Charities soon bore rich fruit, and numerous religious organizations and individuals enthusiastically jumped on board, all eager to help the starving babies of Biafra. Offers of monetary and material assistance poured in from organizations around the globe: there were the American Jewish Emergency Effort for Biafran Relief; the American Committee to Keep Biafra Alive; the Committee for Nigeria/Biafra Relief, based on the campus of Harvard University, and the United Nations Children's Fund, to name just four.

But the Nigerian government refused to allow a direct airlift to Biafra, concerned about the smuggling of weapons, while the Biafran government refused to accept any shipments directly from Nigeria, fearing that the foodstuffs could be poisoned. Meanwhile, children and the elderly continued to die in the wake of the political stalemate.

| Chapter 14 | **A PLAN IS HATCHED TO WHISK MY FAMILY OUT OF BIAFRA** |
|---|---|

One morning after mass in early 1969, Sister Mary Thomas handed me a letter, and I immediately recognized Christopher's handwriting. Unbelievable! Then I noticed the return address on the envelope, and instantly my heart began to pound, and I could hardly wait to tear it open to find out the details. Somehow, my letter had found its way to Christopher, who was now living in the United States of America. America! Christopher had been at Fourah Bay in Sierra Leone. How did he get to America? All these thoughts whirled in my head as I gazed at the unopened letter.

When I saw my husband's penmanship, I experienced a tumultuous rush of emotions that I could not put into words. My biggest relief at this point was that Christopher at least knew we were alive, and I knew he, too, was alive and well. But living in America? How did he get there? America was truly far-fetched in my imagination, but my joy was unsurpassed. I dropped on my knees in gratitude to God for blessing the efforts of an Irish nun in locating my husband, and making it possible for me to know that he was safe where he was. But his living in America was startling to me. That was not on our agenda when he left us to attend Fourah Bay

University in Sierra Leone. How had our collective dream of going overseas materialized for Christopher alone? For a while, I was torn between being happy to hear from him and being somewhat depressed that he had gone overseas without me, but all these thoughts vanished as soon as I opened the letter.

I did not immediately open the letter, deciding instead to suspend my curiosity and rush home to check on my children. When I had a moment to collect my thoughts, I gingerly opened the envelope containing the soft paper on which the letter had been handwritten, and learned Christopher also had been searching for me. He explained that because of the war, returning to Biafra was not an option after he graduated from Fourah Bay University. But the omens were in his favor, for he applied for and was offered a scholarship under the auspices of the United States Agency for International Development (USAID), and subsequently traveled to the United States on a student visa in the fall of 1967. He enrolled at Northwestern University in Evanston, Illinois, to earn a post graduate degree in finance. Still thinking that the crisis would soon end, his plan was to send for us in 1968, but the war had dragged on and lasted longer than anyone could have imagined. Christopher wrote that he had been deeply worried about us, and had been struggling in school as a result.

He also narrated how he had been introduced to a group of Americans by his mentor and professor, Dr. Peter Dietz, the dean of Northwestern University's School of Business. Dr. Dietz was concerned that Christopher's apparent distraction was affecting his academic performance, and thought that if he had some acquaintance with a few Americans, he might begin to feel more relaxed and focus better on his studies.

Christopher further stated that over the course of several months, he had shared his story with Dr. Dietz, his wife Betty, and their close friends, Don and Janet Nevins, and Jim and Helen Wolter, all of whom he sometimes shared Friday night dinners with. Christopher had confided in them that he did not know the fate of his wife and children, from whom he had not heard since leaving them in August of 1966. He noted that although Dr. Dietz's friends had been very kind and thoughtful, the reports of the carnage happening in Biafra had led everyone to fear the worst. They had initially tried to convince Christopher to accept that his entire family may have perished in the war, based on all of the gloomy media reports on Biafra. They had even suggested that Christopher marry a fellow Nigerian girl, who was also studying at Northwestern University.

But Christopher could not be convinced that his family was gone, confident in the knowledge that his wife was strong and resilient, and would attempt to beat all odds to keep her family alive. When his new friends could not convince Christopher to move on without knowing the fate of his family, all of whom had been presumed dead, they began to explore other ways in which they might be able to help him.

I smiled when I read what Christopher had written about me, delighted that, despite our prolonged absence from each other, he still believed in me, and still wanted to be with his family. By the grace of God, we were alive and safe, even though the situation in Biafra had begun to degenerate into a dire emergency. Death was all around us, and neither I nor anyone else in Biafra could predict what the future held.

Christopher's total conviction that his family was still alive became an incentive for the group to begin making an elaborate plan to locate me and my children, and possibly whisk us out of Biafra. They knew that this plan was not going to be easy, but they were prepared to try. And to further boost their morale, the arrival of my letter, detailing our survival strategies, seemed to confirm to his friends what Christopher had been telling them about me. In November of 1968, during Thanksgiving dinner at the home of Dean Dietz and his wife, Betty, the group came up with the final details of the plan.

In addition to the Dietzs, the Nevins and the Wolters, the group had expanded to include Jim and Pat Crisman of Glenview and David and Margo Krupp of Highland Park, Illinois. Their first line of action had been to reach out to congregations at the local Catholic and Presbyterian churches, and several Jewish synagogues, and get them involved in the mission.

\* \* \* \* \*

Years later, Janet Nevins would recount for me her memories of those events, sharing the background and details of the plan the couples had hatched in 1968, that ultimately became the framework for their efforts to save the lives of my family. Below is an excerpt from her story:

*We were first friends with Peter and Betty Dietz, and then I met Helen Wolter. Along with our husbands, all six of us became friends. Betty and I always loved to get together and cook, and we would all have dinner together. We just had a lot of fun.*

*Peter was a professor at Northwestern and he taught graduate students. He was an expert in pension funds, incidentally. He taught students in the MBA program and Chris was in one or two of his classes.*

*One evening we were all together and Peter said, "There's this nice man in my class and he says he's from Biafra. There's a war there and he seems so lonely and isolated, and I feel for him. He seems to be alone here in Chicago."*

*We all talked about it and agreed to invite Chris out with us on the following Friday night or Saturday night. I don`t know who said it, but I remember the sentiment being: "Let's bring him out and see what we can do to cheer him up, and let him get to know some Americans."*

*Since we thought of ourselves as average Americans, we felt that Chris might feel comfortable with us. So we invited him to one of our Friday night dinners, and he came over to the Dietz's house. Chris was such a lovely man; so sweet. He just had, you could just tell, he had such a lovely soul.*

*Over time, Chris eventually admitted to having Angelina as a wife. About two dinners later, we finally got him to admit that he had one child. And every weekend from then on, another child would be revealed, until we realized that for heaven's sake, his wife Angelina was in Africa in the middle of a war with six children all by herself!*

*We all started talking at once, saying how terrible the situation was. It was now obvious that Chris was just worrying himself sick about the plight of his family. I'm not sure who spoke up first, but before the night was over we agreed that we had to do something about it.*

*In those days, we had the "Yankee can-do" mentality. We all put our heads together and decided that we had to find a way to get Chris' family out of Africa. I was in the background during this part of the planning. This is where*

121

*people who knew more about the world, politics and such, began talking about what needed to be done. I even overheard them say something about finding a pilot and a plane to get Chris' family out of Biafra. That's when we realized how difficult this effort was going to be. We were going to have to raise a great deal of money.*

*Peter, Jim and Don began speaking at any church or synagogue willing to have them. They told these congregations that they were appealing for funds to rescue a family from the Biafran War and get them to the United States. These men went to as many houses of worship in the Chicago area that would give them time to speak. And my gosh, they got people interested! There was some publicity in the press and the campaign started to take shape. Money actually started coming in, and we realized, "Wow, maybe we can do this thing!" We really got excited.*

* * * * *

Christopher's letter from the U.S. contained very detailed instructions about the plans he and his American friends had developed for our family's escape from Biafra. The group had also enlisted the support of U.S. Congressman Ab Mikva and U.S. Senator Charles Percy. Involving these two lawmakers took the group over a big hump. Despite a cap on the quota of Biafran refugees that could be allowed to immigrate to the U.S., Rep. Mikva and Senator Percy successfully made a case to Congress to make our family the exception, appealing to its members to recognize the dire implication of our plight in Biafra. The lawmakers' timely intervention made us eligible to apply for emergency U.S. visas. As soon as my husband's friends received word that the U.S. government had cleared us to travel, they began to work with Biafran officials to iron out the final details of our departure, and paid the air fare for the seven of us.

Christopher had indicated in his letter that I needed to get started right away. First, I had to obtain the exit permits from the Biafran government, which had been pre-arranged and presumably paid for by my husband's American friends. These permits were to be issued personally by the Biafran commander, Lt. Col. Odumegwu Ojukwu, who had been contending with enemy fire in Umuahia, Biafra's capital at that time. It is noteworthy that as the Nigerian troops continued to attack and overrun Biafran cities and villages, the size of Biafra continued to shrink, and each time the seat of government was affected the capital would be moved to a safer location. At the time we were preparing to leave, Umuahia was the capital.

This was a daunting task, but I had to figure out how to safely get to Ojukwu in the midst of the war. As I prayed for the courage and wisdom to take the right steps, I did my best to ignore Christopher's closing words of warning: "This may or may not work." I had reached the conclusion that with the escalation of fighting and the incessant air raids all over Biafra, the sentence "This may or may not work" was not an option at all.

* * * * *

My resolve to do my best to facilitate our departure notwithstanding, I was further awakened to the ominous reality of our existence in Biafra in February of 1969, when the Nigerian troops bombed the big market located between Owerri and Mbaise, not too far from the site of the current Imo International Airport. Because of the blockade and limited opportunities for the relief planes to land, the market had been swarming with people in search of food. Suddenly incendiary bombs began to rain from the sky, terrorizing everyone in the market and causing a great stampede. By the time the chaos was over, at least 300 people—mostly women and children—had been mangled beyond recognition, their scorched bodies scattered throughout the length and breadth of the marketplace. Those who narrowly escaped the carnage returned to the village to tell the story of the attack, the gory details etched in their memory forever.

Within days of the market attack, there were rumors that the Nigerian army was about to overrun Mbaise, one of the few remaining strongholds of Biafra, and our ancestral hometown. Everybody was in panic, but fortunately, it did not happen, but the fear all around was palpable. Biafrans were still hopeful that the outside world, particularly the West, would offer some form of help by way of military support or weapons, but that help did not come. With the exception of Ivory Coast, Gabon, Zambia, and Tanzania, as well as a small band of mercenaries committed to our cause, Biafrans were largely left to their own devices. Whatever little help we received was not enough to protect our infant nation.

* * * * *

Amidst all of the carnage and chaos, I remained confident that it was God's plan that my children and I would soon get out of Biafra. Sister Mary Thomas's suggestion that I send a letter to Christopher had set in motion an endless machinery of miracles to come my way, triggering off a chain of happy events, and ensuring that no obstacles reared their ugly heads until God's plan for me had come to fruition. While I was reconnecting with my husband by mail, God was shedding His grace on Christopher's friends and mentors in the United

States. These kind strangers, united in their mission to save an African family from certain death, had devoted time, made monetary contributions, and taken great risks to help us. Surely, their actions were a measure of their humanity because they had not hoped to get anything in return. They neither knew us nor hoped to make a name for themselves for their sole intention was to "save lives for the glory of God."

Every now and again, I would wonder anew about certain events in my life, and would think about the circuitous routes Christopher's letters and mine had traveled to get to us. Christopher's letter had traveled from the U.S. to Ireland, and Gabon, and had been smuggled from Gabon into Biafra in the midst of a raging civil war. I knew all this was God's design, and that was the proof I needed to know that my family would be rescued.

| Chapter 15 | **EFFORTS TO OBTAIN EXIT PERMITS FROM THE COMMANDER OF THE BIAFRAN ARMED FORCES** |
|---|---|

In preparation to leave Biafra, I turned over the operation of the refugee food center to Naomi Eke, a trustworthy woman in our village, and gave away all of my family's belongings. On April 15, 1969, I gathered my children and hired a truck to take us the six miles to Umuahia, the seat of the Biafran government, to obtain our travel permits. I had hoped that as soon as we obtained our travel permits my family would head straight to the makeshift airstrip at Uli, known as Uli Airport, to catch that evening's Caritas International flight, since we could fly out by any available plane.

Looking back now, I shudder at how anyone could hope to carry out such an ambitious and adventurous plan, given that we would still need to hire a truck to take us to the airport, which was about 60 miles away. Somehow I was determined that we would take that chance, even though air raids had been rampant around the area because of the airstrip and the numerous military camps located in the surrounding villages.

When the truck that took us to Umuahia dropped us off at the end of Okpara Road, the location of the seat of the

Biafran government, I left my children under a cashew tree some 50 feet from the building, and went inside to wait in line behind the scores of people waiting to see the Biafran military commander, Lt. Col. Odumegwu Ojukwu.

Just before it got to my turn to see him, the enemy troops began bombing Umuahia. The room immediately erupted in screams and people ran for cover. Suddenly, Ojukwu's office door swung open and an aide yelled to him: "Sir, the Nigerians have entered Umuahia!"

I watched as Ojukwu grabbed his gun, shoved it in its holster and rushed out from his office. He and his staff immediately fled through the back door and jumped into a waiting jeep. I learned later that the Nigerian troops were about 10 miles away, at a place called Uzuakoli. There had been a general concern that the enemy troops were intent on capturing Ojukwu, and that would mean the end of the war and the ultimate defeat.

I quickly snapped out of my shock and dashed back to the cashew tree where I had left my children, and we all huddled together on the ground and prayed as the shelling raged. Suddenly, an explosive fell right in front of us, creating a gaping hole, but did not explode. Because a heavy rain had fallen the night before, the ground was soft and muddy, which possibly had caused the bomb to penetrate deeply into the soil. For a moment, my mind flashed back to the other bomb that had fallen in front of me as I took cover on a cassava mound near our village. This incident was another evidence of God's intervention in my hour of need because it was His grace that protected me and my children from imminent death!

My children were so brave, despite their young ages, and

I was surprised they did not yell and scream during the attack, but remained calm the entire time.

All of those people who had come to see Ojukwu ran for cover in all directions, and thankfully, no one hiding near us had been killed, but the pandemonium and screams of so many terrified and injured people seemed to be as lethal as the bombs. When the attack had ceased and the screams of terror had subsided, the cries for help rent the air, and I suddenly realized that it was getting dark and I had to get my children to safety. Our only option now was to return home to Okwu village.

Desperate and confused, I eventually hailed a kind and compassionate truck driver who was willing to take me and my children back to Okwu Nguru. During the drive home, I tried not to think about the disaster that could have been our plight that day, but I still thought about other serious matters. Not only had I given away our belongings in anticipation of our departure, our home was no longer the refugee center, meaning we no longer had ready access to food.

Christopher's mother Janet, unaware of our plight, and thinking we had already left for Uli Airport, became distraught when she saw us. All she wanted was for me and my children to have a safe passage out of Biafra. We spent the next two months in the village, a period that recorded our most difficult struggles during the Biafran war. Since hunger had been the greatest weapon Nigeria had used against Biafra, I realized my entire family was right in the line of fire. So I began to send my eldest children to join the throngs of other hungry children in the village in making the rounds to area refugee centers, standing in long lines under the scorching heat or pouring rain in hopes of securing food for our family. As far as the refugee centers went, there were good and bad days; good days meant that my children would come home with a little supply of food, while bad days implied they would come home with nothing at all.

* * * * *

By late May of 1969, when I had gathered enough momentum to make a second attempt to get the exit permits from Lt. Col. Ojukwu, the seat of government had been moved to Okigwe, a town located more than 30 miles away from our home. I had reckoned that at that point in the war, it was unsafe to attempt to travel by truck, and my only option was to walk the distance. I had calculated it would take me at least three days to get to my destination.

I finally departed for Okigwe from Okwu Nguru, leaving a tearful Janet at home with the children. On the way, I purchased a coconut for a penny, and picked up several ripe mangoes and papayas, also known as "paw-paws," that had fallen from wild trees blooming in profusion along my route. I hoped the fruit would sustain me through my journey to Okigwe.

Because of the war, it was not uncommon to find women walking by themselves on the roads because most able-bodied men and boys had been drafted to fight for Biafra. But the women knew to be wary of the soldiers, who were greatly feared because of their propensity to menace and harass civilians, particularly women. These frustrated soldiers would sometimes seize women, mostly young girls, on the road or forcibly take them from their homes, and carry them off to their camps and rape them. Food was equally scarce for the soldiers who would readily seize and kill any chickens and goats within sight for food. Personally, I was not afraid because my strong faith in God had been the pillar on which

I always anchored, even though I still ducked out of sight whenever I heard the sound of or saw a military vehicle.

\* \* \* \* \*

At night, I stayed at refugee camps, and it was during one of those stays that I ran into a former colleague, Elizabeth Effiong, with whom I taught at Cornelia Connelly College, Afaha Oku, Uyo. For the first few minutes of our reunion, we wept on each other's shoulders, both of us relieved to see a familiar face, and to still be alive. Before we parted, she told me she was worried about not having an *Ichafu* or head wrap. The *Ichafu* is an ancient cultural tradition and an integral part of all African married women's attire, and women felt incomplete without one.

To ease my former colleague's concern, I took off my own scarf from my head and tore it in half and gave her a piece. We hugged again before I left the camp, continuing my journey. Years later, I would think about how even in the midst of the war, the *Ichafu* remained a symbol of strength and beauty for two Biafran women, an aspect of our traditional dress that had helped us to veil our feelings of vulnerability and powerlessness. That encounter raised my consciousness to the symbolic nature of the *Ichafu*, as every Biafran woman I encountered had her *Ichafu* gracefully draped around her head. Women in rural communities also used the *Ichafu* as a protective gear by tying it around their waist to secure their wrapper, a strategy that prevents their being stripped naked should a fight ensue. I saw this piece of our native attire as symbolic of the stamina, fortitude and courage of my fellow country women who were determined not to be intimidated by war.

\* \* \* \* \*

By the time I arrived at Okigwe after three days, I was fatigued and weary, and had to find a place to rest before attempting to start looking for Lt. Col. Ojukwu's government office. Because of security concerns, I deemed it unwise to ask anyone on the street about the location of Ojukwu's office. There were too many saboteurs—people disloyal to the Biafran cause—who would gladly betray the leader at whim for a small amount of money. I had come this far only to realize I had no clue about how to get to Ojukwu's office, but I was confident that the good Lord in His infinite mercy would be my guide.

As I was resting on a large rock, an Army jeep stopped nearby, and I looked up and heard someone call, "Sister?" I was surprised to see Christina Eñeremadu, a nurse and a dear friend, whom I had known for many years, dressed in military fatigues. Her medical background had apparently made her an asset to the Biafran Army, and from the stripes on her sleeves, I could see that she had risen to the rank of Captain. As we talked, I learned she had volunteered to join the medical personnel who were responsible for caring for the wounded Biafran soldiers.

"You are far away from Okwu," she said. "How did you get here?"

"I have been walking for the past three days," I replied.

"Without shoes or boots?" She asked

"Yes, of course," I answered.

Christina began to cry, and despite my best efforts not to cry too, my own tears flowed effortlessly. The trip had taken a bigger toll on me than I could imagine, and I had not yet achieved my goal. I did not share my reason for coming to Okigwe with Christina, and neither did she ask, but I knew it was safe to ask her for directions about how to get to Ojukwu. She gave me directions, albeit discreetly, on how to get to Ojukwu's office, enjoining on me the necessity for discretion, but could not offer me a ride.

"I am sorry, Sister," she said sadly. "Regulations prohibit me from driving you there."

I nodded my head. I completely understood her situation.

"But I can tell you how to walk there," she said with a shy smile. "It is not too far."

Then she got in the jeep and her driver drove off, leaving me as I waved her goodbye in gratitude. Christina had become my guardian angel on this very day! I carefully followed her directions, which I had already memorized, until I arrived at the camouflaged Biafran government premises. The place was well concealed beneath the trees on a palm plantation, and as I walked round the trees to the building I was relieved to see a small group of women, Ojukwu's special aides, and once again felt God's protection. I quickly realized I knew Ojukwu's secretary and a few of his aides, two of whom were Sylvester Okeahialam and Austin Okafor, a brother-in-law to my friend Nelly Okafor.

Although it was nearly the end of their workday, the women warmly welcomed me, and were curious to know my reason for making such a risky journey from Okwu Nguru to Okigwe. When I explained that I had walked for three days from my village to their office, they graciously offered me food and water, and offered me accommodation at the plantation for the night. Although neither of them inquired about the nature of my business with Lt. Col. Ojukwu, they gave me tips on what to do to be the first person in line the next morning to see the military commander. In spite of the remoteness of this make shift office, those who needed to see the Head of the Biafran Government for important issues still sought him out.

I was physically exhausted, but felt exhilarated and relieved. I knelt down and prayed in gratitude to God that my family's ordeal would soon be over. I was not sure I would be able to sleep, but I laid down on the camp bed the women had provided for me. My bed was in the open, and I deeply breathed in the cool night air under the palm trees. The grounds were as quiet as a cemetery, and there was no light to pierce the thick, scary darkness that enveloped the entire place.

In the morning, I once again experienced tremendous hospitality from the women, having been offered both a bath and breakfast. When it was time for Ojukwu to begin seeing visitors, I was immediately ushered in. The military leader was seated at a table, and setting eyes on him I thought he looked quite thin, unlike the burly, young officer I had seen on television much earlier in the war. Like all Biafrans, the war had taken a toll on him as well.

"Lt. Col. Ojukwu, I am Angelina Ihejirika," I said.

"What may I do for you, Mrs. Ihejirika?"

"My husband Christopher had written in his letter to me that his American friends had arranged with you to give exit permits to me and my children. My husband told me that if I mentioned this to you, you would definitely understand what I was talking about."

Ojukwu looked at me briefly, and nodded his head, and taking out seven pieces of paper, carefully wrote out instructions on them, and signed each of them, and handed them to me, his expression unchanged.

"God bless you," I said to him, and immediately took my first baby steps to freedom, and resuming the long walk back home.

Somehow, Ojukwu had already met with the Peter Dietz's group in New York during one of his incognito travels to the U.S. in search of aid to sustain and help win the war. Ojukwu had communicated to them that the only way my children and I could leave the country was if I picked up the permits in person. That was why I made the first futile trip to Umuahia, and walked for three days to Okigwe to collect the permits. My meeting with Ojukwu had opened the door for our passage to the United States, and to freedom.

# Chapter 16 ARRIVAL IN THE UNITED STATES

I left Okigwe as soon as I got the exit permits, and secured them by wrapping them in my outer wrapper and tucking it in my blouse so that the heavy rains would not destroy the precious permits. I traveled home by foot the same way I had come, without stopping at the different refugee camps. I did not want anyone to ask me where I had been or why I had gone there.

The last leg of my trip was the scariest of the entire saga. In addition to the heavy rain, I had to walk in the dark, lonely night all by myself. On both sides of the narrow roads were thick forests and family burial grounds. I was cold and wet, frightened by every thunder clap and lightning bolt, and imagined dead people emerging from their graves and coming after me. I regularly looked behind me to make sure no one was following me. All during this journey, I had one hand tightly clutching and protecting the wrapper that held our precious permits, while I used the other hand to constantly make the sign of the cross.

\* \* \* \* \*

My mother-in-law Janet was anxiously waiting on the

veranda when I walked into our compound. "Mama, what are you doing sitting up so late at night peering into the darkness and watching this very heavy rain," I asked her quietly so as to de-emphasize any excitement about my return.

"Every evening for the past six days, after putting the children to bed, I would sit in my easy chair, praying and looking out for you," Janet told me as we embraced, both of us heaving a heavy sigh of relief.

We were so happy to be reunited, basking not only in the joy of our common love for Christopher, but also recognizing the special bond of our collective womanhood. I wished my mother-in-law had been willing to travel with us to America because I was sure Christopher would continue to worry about her wellbeing when we leave. I was quite certain I could have convinced Lt. Col. Ojukwu to issue me one more permit to accommodate Janet, but she had told me before I departed for Okigwe that her home was in Biafra, and she would rather stay behind. I felt better when I remembered that Janet's daughter, Katherine, would be around and happy to care for her mother, along with her own children.

"Angelina," she said, "Live as happily with your husband and your children in America as you did in the North."

It was then that I shared my good news with Janet by whispering in her ear, "I got the exit permits from Ojukwu."

She suddenly hugged me tightly.

"You should go to bed," I said, gently releasing myself from Janet's embrace. "I need to do so myself. We will talk more in the morning. Goodnight,

Mama."

I tiptoed to my room, hoping to fall asleep as soon as possible, but the excitement of our new reality kept me awake all night. I still got up early the following morning, knocked on Janet's door to tell her, and left for morning mass as usual.

After mass, I waited for the nuns to finish their prayers in the chapel, and when they came out, I approached Sister Mary Thomas.

"Sister, it is done," I said.

Sister Mary Thomas was ecstatic and took me to the parlor to share the happy news with the other nuns. After that, I walked home to my children. Their grandmother had already told them of my success with Ojukwu, and they were eagerly waiting for me.

"Will these papers take us to see our father?" one of my children asked.

"Yes," I replied.

"When are we leaving, Mommy?" another chimed in.

"Soon," I replied. "Very soon."

\* \* \* \* \*

A day before we planned to make our escape, the Nigerian troops intensified their efforts in blocking the arrival of the relief flights to Biafra. They had shot down a Swedish relief plane on June 5, 1969, before it could land at Uli Airport, the makeshift landing strip used for delivering food and medical supplies shipments provided by international aid agencies. Everyone on board the plane was killed. The Nigerian government considered the airstrip illegal, claiming it was being used to smuggle weapons into

Biafra, and expressed no remorse for taking down the plane. Sadly, such tragedies were rarely publicly denounced and publicized, but often discussed only in hushed tones for fear of demoralizing both the Biafran army and the civilians.

Uli Airport had been designated as my family's escape route. Unaware of the relief plane's disaster, which had occurred a day after my return from Okigwe, I moved ahead with my plans to leave Biafra. My younger brother, Sylvester, a mechanical engineer, worked at the fuel directorate and was stationed near a village named Amandugba, a short distance from the Uli Airport.

Sylvester knew about all of our arrangements to leave Biafra, and I had arranged with him to send a driver on the evening of June 5, 1969, to pick us up at our home and take us to the airport. Christopher had specified in his letter that I bring just a few of my native attire and only a change of clothes for each of the children. Going by my husband's instruction, I packed our clothing in a raffia bag instead of a suit case to make it easier to carry. I gave away the rest of our belongings to the people we were leaving behind.

My second son Francis had insisted on bringing his own empty raffia bag to serve as a memento, something that would always remind him of his homeland. I brought the rosary beads that Sister Mary Thomas had given me for each of my children, along with a prayer book that the nun had lovingly presented to me.

After we all got in the car, Sylvester's driver had to drive without headlights for about an hour across treacherous, war-torn terrain. The headlights could attract unwanted attention, including that of Nigerian war planes laden with bombs. All the while, I clutched my rosary beads and prayed to God to protect and guide us safely to Uli Airport.

Thankfully, we arrived in Amandugba without incident. Sylvester then raced against the clock to take us to Uli Airport, which was hidden deep within a dense forest. My brother had already made arrangements for us to hide out in a bunker, which had been dug for the airport workers, until the plane arrived. He took it upon himself to cuddle my youngest daughter Rosemary in order to keep the toddler quiet and settled while we awaited the arrival of the plane.

As soon as we heard the rumbling of the plane's engines, we were instructed to scramble as fast as we could to the runway. Because there would be many people unloading the supplies from the plane, as soon as it had been emptied the plane would take off immediately so as to avoid detection by Nigerian war planes searching for the relief planes to shoot them down. We had to be in the position to rush up to the loading ramp, and we were more than ready to get on board.

I hugged Sylvester and whispered "thank you" as I took charge of my youngest daughter. Fighting back tears, I took the extended hand of the pilot who helped me to board the plane, and I remember his telling me that he was an Israeli. I would always remember that he had a kind face, a calm voice, and a patient demeanor. I would always be grateful that he was equally very friendly to my sons. Since that day, I have had a soft spot in my heart for Israel, in appreciation of those brave Israeli pilots who flew in food and supplies to Biafra under extremely dangerous conditions, and because Israel was among the first to have the courage to assist Biafra after the secession.

This plane was a cargo plane, not a passenger plane with rows of seats for passengers, so there were only benches bolted in parallel lines to the plane's walls. My family sat close together, and I continued to pray as the plane taxied down the short runway. We were headed to Gabon, one of the few African nations that had recognized and supported Biafra's right to sovereignty.

Not too long after we had been airborne, I heard what sounded like gunfire. As I wondered about what those sounds might be, the pilot invited me into the cockpit, and looking out of the window, I saw people hunched around blazing, open fires. The pilot told me they were Nigerian soldiers shooting at our plane, but assured me that our plane was almost out of the Nigerian airspace, and the weaponry they were using was not powerful enough to reach us.

I did not feel as confident as the pilot, however, and when I returned to my children, I held the baby close to my heart, and directed the rest to snuggle up and hold each other. Once again, I prayed for God's protection and mercy, and implored Him to guide the pilot to safety, away from the ravages of the war we were leaving behind.

* * * * *

Although it was illegal for Biafrans to leave the country, some people's collective goodwill and resources opened doors for us. The kindness of those people who took it upon themselves to help Christopher rescue his family from the ravages of war was beyond my comprehension. These people meticulously made all of the arrangements for my children and me to escape from Biafra, and paid for our flight to the International Airport in Libreville, Gabon, where representatives of the Biafran government were waiting to assist us with our next transfer. The Biafran officials drove us to our accommodations at a nearby hotel and treated us to a feast of our native foods. No one could possibly imagine how happy we were to sit down to eat a well-cooked, sumptuous meal without fear or anxiety of air raids.

Thereafter, we were encouraged by the Biafran officials to rest until it was time for our next flight, which was to Lisbon. For the first time in two years, we went to bed relaxed and without the constant, overhead rumbling of airplane engines.

The next morning, we took a Pan Am Airlines flight to Lisbon, Portugal. Upon arrival, we were again shuttled to a nearby hotel that had already been arranged and paid for through the fundraising efforts of Christopher's friends in the United States. Christopher had instructed me to go to the American Embassy in Lisbon, and the Biafran officials in Gabon readily gave me directions on how to get there. This would be the final hurdle — going to the embassy to present the exit permits I had been guarding closely for entry visas to the United States.

Because of an unexpected delay at the U.S. Embassy, my initial concern was that this snag could mean we might be detained in Lisbon for an unknown period of time. But within a day, our paperwork had been completed, and as soon as I secured our U.S. visas, we were immediately transported to the airport.

All this while, everything seemed surreal to me; we had just left Biafra and were headed to the U.S. All my history and geography lessons notwithstanding, I had no idea where the U.S. was located in the world map.

* * * * *

We arrived in New York on June 9, 1969, and I recall that it was a bright, sunny day. We were met by Dr. Dietz and his wife Betty, who were accompanied by their two children and his parents. There was a layover period before the final leg of our journey to Chicago, where we would be reunited with Christopher. The five families who had helped Christopher—I would prefer to call them American philanthropists—had taken care of every possible detail of our journey. Dr. Dietz had come to New York to ensure we had somewhere to stay during the layover period between flights. Upon arrival, we were driven to the home of Dr. Dietz's parents, who welcomed us like family, making sure we were safe and comfortable at every turn.

After treating us to good food, the Dietzs drove us back to the airport in time to catch the flight to Chicago. I have never ceased to be in awe of these generous and noble people, who will eternally remain a marvel of goodness, and I bless the memories of those of them who have already passed on.

The last leg of the flight was very emotional for me. I knew that within a few hours the dream of reuniting with my husband would finally become a reality. The war had changed me and changed my children, but I was determined that its effects would not forever scar our lives.

At this point in our journey, my children and I had boarded a plane four times, starting at Uli Airport to Gabon, and from there to Lisbon, and then to New York, and now from New York to our final destination, Chicago. At long last, we were headed to Chicago, the city that would be our new home.

\* \* \* \* \*

Christopher was standing on the runway when we disembarked in Chicago, but he was not alone. There were representatives of the various organizations that had helped to bring us to the United States, along with throngs of radio, television and newspaper reporters.

I will never forget the moment that the children and I fell into the embrace of their father. Although our first embrace was brief, all of the challenges, and worries that we had had to overcome to be reunited with him quickly vanished. For a while, it felt surreal, like an event playing out in a dream, but my heart was filled with gratitude to God for bringing my family together again.

The waiting reporters briefly interviewed Christopher and me, asking us how it felt to be reunited with each other and with our entire family, and asking me specifically how it felt to be in the United States. I told the truth and admitted that it felt surreal, like a dream, and I had no words to adequately express my emotions which were at that point threatening to overwhelm me. I said that I knew about Europe, but did not know much about the United States, and would never have imagined that I would be here, particularly under the circumstances. In his turn, Christopher acknowledged that words had failed him, but expressed sentiments similar to mine about the excitement of reuniting with his family.

The interviews over, we left in a motorcade to a community called Northbrook. We then pulled into a brick home where we were informed that we would live in Dean Dietz's home while he and his family were on vacation. Inside the beautifully decorated home, we found two refrigerators filled with a variety of food, and splendidly prepared rooms for our now family of eight to sleep in. I will never forget the curious feeling I had as I walked down the stairs to the basement, the concept of having rooms underground being entirely novel to us. I had never seen basements in Nigerian homes, and even though times and fortunes have changed for many people over there, only a few people have homes with basements.

My children were very happy to sit on the swing and play around in the Dietz's backyard. I envisioned that sooner or later they would begin to act like children once again, carefree and joyful. Not long after our arrival, a plane was flying overhead, and suddenly my children began to scramble, screaming and taking cover, a sad reminder of our Biafran experience. Both Christopher and I ran to them, hugging each one of them, and assuring them that the flying airplanes were friendly and would never hurt them.

"These planes do not have bombs like the Nigerian planes that harassed us in Biafra," I told them. "These ones are just like the airplanes that transported us from Biafra to America. There is nothing to worry about any more, my children," I said.

A few days after settling at the Dietz's residence in Northbrook, Illinois, all of us were taken to the Evanston Hospital for thorough medical check-ups, as part of the five kind couples' philanthropic package for my family, precious gifts that had been meticulously put together even before our arrival.

My own medical assessment was performed by a team of doctors who already knew my story from the media reports. They were extremely thorough and professional during the medical exams, and followed up on all my lab tests.

Surprisingly, I was the only one out of the seven of us who had malaria. The six children were malaria-free, even though they looked quite emaciated due to malnutrition, but were allowed to return to the Northbrook home. I was admitted in the isolation unit of the hospital, having gone through all the formalities of a hospital admission.

The children could not understand why I had to remain in the hospital because they did not believe I was ill, never having seen me sick in all of their young lives. Back home, it was the children themselves who had been prone to sickness from time to time, including suffering from bouts of malaria fever. Seeing me on a hospital bed, and possibly realizing that she may have to go home without me, Rosemary, the baby, started screaming and held on to me. The other children asked their Dad to tell the doctor that "Mama knows how to cure malaria." Christopher watched all that drama as he waited patiently until I was duly settled in my hospital room. After that initial check-up, my husband, Christopher, having now resumed his responsibility as the head of our family, began taking us to our doctors' visits.

Christopher was neither around when I was pregnant nor present when our baby was born, so Rosemary was the one child who did not know her Dad. The two of them had known each other for only the few days we had been in the U.S. And to make matters worse, Christopher called her "Cecilia," the name he had recorded for her on the transit visa, while the rest of us called her Rosemary, the name I gave her at baptism. Rosemary was scared and needed to be convinced that Christopher was her Dad, and that he would take all of them home to eat, and bring them back to me at the hospital. I eventually succeeded in convincing her, and she and the rest of the children left with Christopher for Dean Dietz's home in Northbrook.

I spent almost a week in the hospital because the results of my tests had to be sent to some lab for analysis before the doctors could prescribe the appropriate medications for me.

The nurses drew my blood several times during my admission so much so that I was concerned that what little blood I had was being wasted.

Christopher told me later that the doctors were treating my malaria as an infectious and contagious disease, until he had to explain to them that malaria was an African disease borne by a type of mosquito known as Anopheles, and that all Africans were naturally prone to be afflicted with it from birth.

Christopher told them that back in Nigeria we treated malaria with "Quinine" tablets, which also had a liquid variety. The patient would take four tablets on the first day of treatment, and two tablets every day for the next three days. The 10 tablets taken over four days were considered the full dose for treatment, after which the patient experienced total relief for a long while. Anyway, I was eventually treated and discharged from the hospital, and returned to Northbrook to join my family.

The Sunday after our arrival, we were taken to the United Methodist Presbyterian Church in Northbrook. The community wanted to see and speak with the family from Africa, whom they had worked hard to bring to the United States, and out of the war zone that was Biafra.

We were very warmly received, and as was to be expected, I was bombarded with questions from these people who were curious to hear my responses. Some of the questions they put to me included:

Question: "How were you able to maintain the family and keep the kids safe all by yourself?"

My answer: "I could not have kept the family safe if God had not been my strength." Question: "How did you come to have the faith you have, which is apparent even now?"

My answer: "I was born into a very strong, Christian Catholic family, and above all, I was educated by Irish and American nuns who instilled discipline in me and great faith in Our Lord Jesus Christ, and I have held on to that faith ever since; I do not know what I could have done without it."

One question had stuck with me to this day, and it goes thus:

Question: "What do you intend to do in the long run when you and your family have settled down and joined the American mainstream?"

My answer: First, I am going to work hard to help Christopher to raise our children here. Second, I am determined to do my best to make sure that my family does not become a burden to the society. In addition, I intend to focus my attention, as soon as I am able, on helping others in need.

We stayed in Northbrook for two weeks, just when Dean Dietz's family vacation was about over, and the family would have to return to their home. But the families that brought my family from Biafra had also made arrangements for an apartment large enough for my family of eight. So we moved from the Dietz's home to a federally subsidized apartment on the South Side of Chicago known as South Commons, on 27th Street & Indiana. It was so conveniently located that we could not have wished for anything better. The duplex style apartment had four large bedrooms upstairs while the living room and kitchen were downstairs. There was a Jewel's grocery store in the complex, and a restaurant too. A police station was a stone's throw from the apartment complex.

Michael Reese Hospital was only a few blocks away from the building, and our church, St. James Catholic Church, was located just two blocks away, and it had a grade school of which Sister Mary Margaret was the principal. Winifred, Christopher and Francis were enrolled in St James Catholic School, with the exception of Mary Ann and Maudlyne, who attended Dunbar Kindergarten; Rosemary, being too young, was with me at home. Everything was in close proximity to our building, and buses were readily accessible at all times.

Christopher gloatingly told the story of how we came to live in this enviable location since his prior attempts to rent an apartment had been a nightmare. According to him, whenever he made a call about the apartments that had been advertised in the newspapers, the landlord would schedule an appointment with him to see the apartment. But as soon as he showed up that same landlord would turn around and tell him that the apartment had already been taken.

Christopher had been so frustrated by the inconsistency of the landlords that he decided to share his ordeal with one of his benefactors who told Christopher to leave it to him. Having been briefed on the problem, this man then called the landlord to see the apartment that had been denied Christopher, and the apartment suddenly became available. The man returned to Christopher and took him to sign the lease, to the utter dismay of the white landlord. We then moved in and began in earnest to settle in America.

For more than 46 years, we have enjoyed every peaceful day away from the ravages of war, hunger, oppression, and disease, a precious gift that had been given to my family by the goodness of the Almighty Father, the God of glory and majesty, as well as the kindness of total strangers who have blessed my family with their humanity. My heart is filled with gratitude as I continually resoundingly intone: God bless America, and bless those noble families that worked so hard and sacrificed so much to salvage me and my family from the throes of death.

# EPILOGUE

The rolling, green hills of Ireland were once home to thousands of Catholic nuns who became missionaries and voluntarily traveled to Africa during the early days of British colonialism. These were courageous women, many of whom made it to Nigeria in the face of tremendous odds, and claimed it as their home.

They braved the hot, humid climate, relentless mosquitoes, and hostile, skeptical men to make it possible for Nigerian children, especially girls like me, to receive an education. These nuns inspired me to become a teacher and, because of them, I was also able to help thousands of Nigerian girls turn their lives around.

In 2007, I traveled to Ireland from Chicago. As part of my trip, I promised a member of my parish prayer group that I would deliver her note to her sister in-law, who was then living in a nursing home in Dublin. Arriving at the rehabilitation home, I was surprised to learn that all of the residents there had previously worked in Nigeria. When I was taken to the elderly and sick nun's room, she was lying in bed facing the wall.

"My name is Angelina Ihejirika," I said. "I have a card for you from your sister in-law in Chicago."

I handed the card to her attending nurse, who was seated in a chair adjacent to the bed. To everyone's amazement, the elderly nun suddenly turned over to face us.

"Please read it to me," she said to her nurse, barely audible.

I do not recall the contents of the card, but I will always remember the elderly nun's blue eyes as she gazed at me, listening to that message.

"Mrs. Ihejirika, where and how did you meet my sister in-law?" the nun asked.

"I met her in Chicago, Sister. She belongs to one of my prayer groups, which meets every Monday, and when I announced to the group I was going on a pilgrimage to Dublin, she asked me to deliver the card to you."

"Is she alright?" the sick nun asked.

"Yes, she is alright," I replied.

I clasped her hand and said a little prayer for her. The nun then turned back to face the wall, resuming the position in which I initially found her.

On leaving the nun's room, I asked for permission to visit all of the nuns. I was grateful that God had given me the opportunity to personally thank these women for all of the great work they did in Nigeria, especially for all they suffered to educate us. These nuns had endured hot climates and pesky mosquitos undaunted by nets or repellants. To keep us in school, they had to learn to negotiate with reluctant parents and nonchalant elders. Even more difficult, they had to endure the isolation and loneliness of living in a foreign land. Ultimately, it was their faith in God and commitment to their mission that became the source of their courage and joy.

I found some of the nuns seated in wheelchairs, and as they reminisced with me about the old days, tears flowed from their eyes and mine, particularly when the conversation shifted to the Biafran war. For many of them, the war was the only reason they left Nigeria, having been subjected to extreme measures.

I did not burden them with the story of my escape from Biafra, but we focused instead on the joy of our reunion, which coincidentally occurred on the 70th anniversary of the nuns' missionary work in Nigeria. Along with my fellow pilgrims, I joined the nuns in celebration.

* * * * *

Our pilgrimage group was scheduled to head to the holy Knock Shrine in Mayo, Ireland, about 130 miles north east of Dublin, but before we left the rehabilitation home, I learned of another nursing home in Dublin where retired nuns who had previously worked in Nigeria were living. So before we left that part of Ireland, I asked the members of my group if we could pay a brief visit to the Missionary Sisters of the Holy Rosary, who lived at 48 Temple Road, Dartry, Dublin, and they graciously agreed.

We were warmly received by a younger novitiate, who said she would inform the director of the home of our presence. Within minutes of our arrival, I beheld the face of Sister Mary Theodora, the former principal who had recruited me to teach at Owerri Girls' Secondary School. The nun had left Biafra at the beginning of the war, and needless to say that our reunion was bittersweet.

# BUILDING BRIDGES AND ENCOURAGING HOPE

*Voice of a Woman for Humanity* is a nonprofit organization dedicated to battling hunger and poverty, promoting physical health and welfare, and providing educational opportunities for disadvantaged, indigent populations in rural continental Africa, such as Nigeria and Sierra Leone, among others.

The organization was established in 1996 by Angelina N. Ihejirika, an African mother of seven, who barely escaped the bloodshed,  hunger and famine that plagued Biafrans during the Nigeria-Biafra war. She founded the organization after returning to her home village in Nigeria and discovering that the women and children were again being plagued with kwashiokor, an affliction caused by severe malnutrition. This time, the cause was not war, but economic hardship. Mrs. Ihejirika vowed to do whatever she could to change the situation for these women and their children by founding the organization whose motto is: *"As I was saved so shall I save."*

In 1999, the Marian Soup Kitchen in Okwu Nguru in Aboh Mbaise Local Government Area was established under the auspices of *Voice of a Woman for Humanity*, and within a short period of time, the organization had grown from feeding 250 hungry women and children weekly to serving 700. This growth made it imperative that a second kitchen be opened a year later in Egberede-Eziala, where 250 people were fed every week. The organization has since expanded to include five more feeding stations, all in Aboh Mbaise Local Government Area.

Aside from providing food for the needy, the organization installed a bore hole to provide clean, running water to the villagers in Okwu, thereby alleviating the dire problem of water scarcity, particularly during the dry season. Additionally, the organization fulfilled its goal of providing electrical power to the village by installing a giant transformer for that purpose; initiating vocational training for the poor, and providing scholarships for poor village children. These scholarships sponsor candidates from primary through secondary and occupational or tertiary levels, up to the university level. The scholarship program pays for university tuitions, and we have succeeded in producing scores of graduates.

Mrs. Ihejirika's second son, Francis, a pediatrician, recruits dozens of medical doctors and nurses who participate annually in a two-week, volunteer, medical mission to Nigeria, administering health care to the sick and needy at no cost to them.

Since its establishment almost 20 years ago, *Voice of a Woman for Humanity* has distributed clothing, medical and nutritional supplements to the poor. Our future plans include expanding our mission to other African countries. For example, *Voice of a Woman* twice sent monetary and material supplies to Sierra Leone for cholera victims during the civil war, and most recently, the organization provided assistance to the country for Ebola victims. Our primary goal remains to save others as we were saved. A portion of the proceeds from this book will help fund the continuing efforts of *Voice of a Woman for Humanity*.

*Deo Gratias*. Thanks Be to God.


### *Preview of Next Book*

The day our family arrived in Chicago, the *Sun Times* ran a story about us and local television stations ran reports about our family during their 5:00 p.m. and 10:00 p.m. news broadcasts. Our story and pictures have appeared in numerous publications in the Chicago area since then. Over time, we came to the realization that we are in America to stay and that propelled us to undertake the arduous task of joining in the search for the golden fleece, just like other immigrants who have come to the United States in search of a better life.

# GLOSSARY

*Chin-chin*:      Strips of dough baked until crunchy.

*Puff-puff*:      Spongy, deep-fried dough, similar to a donut.

*Garri*:      Grain derived from dried cassava paste.

*Kwashiorkor*:      A potentially fatal condition caused by severe protein deficiency.

*Ichafu*:      Head wrap made of fabric.

# INDEX